C000088441

Management is something most within our career, but few of us a

Anne's easy-to-read style, the handy tips, guides and check contained within this book make it an invaluable guide for anyone starting out in their management career, or experienced managers who want to revisit some core concepts. Like Tracy-Anne herself, it bubbles with insight and energy, and every encounter reveals some new nugget of information. It is a worthwhile addition to any bookshelf.

Neil Lakeland FCIM FInstLM

Thank you Tracy-Anne for such a down-to-earth, practical, accessible book. It is like the go-to handbook for managers, whether newly promoted or the more seasoned variety. I loved the TATTs (Tracy-Anne's Top Tips) in each chapter and the clever references to rugby and what managers can learn from the sport. As an ex-VP of HR, I think this should be compulsory reading in all businesses where people manage teams. This book feels like having a management mentor in my pocket and I wish you had written it years ago when I was floundering as a new manager!

Gill McKay, FCIPD, Neuroscience Trainer and Sobriety Coach and author of the best-selling book 'STUCK: Brain Smart Insights for Coaches'.

The way in which this book is written enables you to dip in and out of it. The chapters are punchy, providing practical tips which are easy to remember and will enable a leader and manager to make change quickly. I like the checklist at the end which seeks to summarise the chapter and provide a "to-do list" of actions to take. A must-read for those who want to be an effective leader and manager.

Karen Martin MBTI RBCB, Director

HOW NOT

TO

BALLS IT UP

A PRACTICAL GUIDE
TO MODERN MANAGEMENT

TRACY-ANNE BARKER

Cover image by: Sam Art Studio
Book design by: SWATT Books Ltd

Printed in the United Kingdom
First Printing, 2022

ISBN: 978-1-7391076-0-4 (Paperback)
ISBN: 978-1-7391076-1-1 (eBook)

Tracy-Anne Barker
Aylesford Kent
ME20 7JQ

www.tabarkerassociates.co.uk

Contents

Foreword

I WILL START this book foreword by introducing myself. I am Kaz Macklin, a comrade collaborator of **Tracy-Anne Barker MCMI. I work for Kent Invicta Chamber of Commerce**

Both Tracy-Anne and I operate in the Kent business community. Tracy-Anne also works with clients across the UK and internationally. I first met the likeable and relatable Tracy-Anne some years ago via a professional introduction. I have watched her business become established and succeed. On meeting Tracy-Anne, over a leisurely latte, I was immediately charmed by her warm and confident approach to her business modeling. Professionally she is absorbing.

Tracy-Anne is one of life's 'givers'. Always open to supporting or helping fellow professionals. She is competently efficient and a tireless advocate for helping others fulfill their potential to improve as an individual and vicariously improve the business they work in. This book is a must for any organisation with teams and a management structure.

Tracy-Anne is uniquely placed, with her vast experience both in the commercial and public sectors. She is a recognised long-standing member of the Chartered Management Institute, with over 25 years of management experience. So, Tracy-Anne really knows her subject matter.

The genesis of the book is Tracy-Anne's conviction in her craft and provides a valuable wealth of information, covering the necessary components to enhance practical modern management practice.

The narrative not only educates but also creates defining junctures on how business managers will from now on view themselves.

The author has adeptly articulated in a subtle and stealthily intelligent way work practices which may sabotage a new manager's success or impede the growth of a more experienced manager who may be struggling, for whatever reason.

For too long there has not been a Little Black Book – Well no more! The author shows us that the sky is now no longer the limit. In sharing pointers and tips, she walks us through how you too can succeed in management, just like her.

The golden age of bygone top-down management styles grounded in the dogmatic approach of carrots and sticks is dispelled. Utilising the management approaches of the first industrial revolution, whilst we are entering a fourth post-Covid industrial revolution creates a paradigm shift. The legacy of the industrial revolution, based on command and control will fence people in, creating sheep. Other approaches seek to understand with brains and hearts and seek purpose, not control. The author's diligent efforts break through in understanding human behaviour and equipping you to be the best you can. Positive mindsets are about creating extraordinary leaders, not ordinary leaders. Teams led by empowering leaders will arguably out-perform others. Good managers move their organisations forwards with happier, more engaged and more productive staff teams. This strengthens relationships and powers an organisation with vision and effectiveness. Win, win.

This is a book for those who dare to ask, "How can I move beyond the outdated management assumptions to a brave new era, and what tools are out there to help me?" The answers lie in 'How Not To Balls it Up'.

I'm serious, this is an enlightening and liberating read for both newly promoted managers and experienced managers who just want to be better and I've not only enjoyed the book but learned many beneficial things from it.

Enjoy!

Kaz Macklin
Area Membership Manager
Kent Invicta Chamber of Commerce

Preface

IF YOU'VE BOUGHT this book, first I would like to say a big thank you. I am by nature quite an introverted person and putting a book together has been a fairly big deal for me.

Secondly, here are some thoughts on who this book is for. If you're relatively new to management or looking to get into management for the first time, or you have been thrown into a management role at the deep end and been given no training, then this is definitely for you. Or it may be that you are more experienced but have run out of ideas on how to develop your management role. Whatever stage you're at in your management career, I guarantee you will find in these pages practical ideas, hints and tips you can implement straightaway. As the title states, you really will learn 'How not to Balls it up' as a manager.

The title and the thinking behind it perhaps need some explaining – it comes from The School of Hard Knocks (of which there are plenty in rugby, but more on that later). It recognises that, out there in the real world, far from looking at things from a 'How to Be a Perfect Manager' stance, life in business and management is all about coping with tough situations and ensuring that things aren't ballsed up. That does *not* mean that this book is in any way negative or focuses just on the Balls ups. BUT it doesn't shy away from looking at the difficult stuff managers need to handle, with loads of real-world examples, and then gives you the ideas and strategies needed to handle things. In the pressurised, fast-moving world of work, if as a manager, at the end of each year you can stand back and say, "You know what, it's been tough, but I didn't Balls it up", then that demonstrates far more realism, courage, determination and grit than saying, "Ooh, I think I'm now the Perfect Manager". Because, you know what, you'll then pick yourself up and start all over again, and the attitude and techniques in this book will help you on that journey.

I always believed having a 'go-to' book like a Manager's Toolkit would have been great when I was working through the management ranks. And it's this belief that has driven me to use all my experiences and put together this book.

When I was starting as a manager, I could have done with a book just like **THIS!**

It's been written in a way that allows you to dip in and dip out as and when the topics or areas of interest arise. It doesn't need to be read in the order of the chapters, it's way more versatile than that. The choice is yours, to help you develop your management skills.

There are checklists, key pointers, and toolkits for you to implement in your role. I have also chosen to share a few of my favourite rugby quotes, and these are peppered throughout the book – you can read more about my love of rugby in Chapter 1.

Throughout the book, I share snippets and stories of my journey through management. There are examples of where things went wrong, and how I put them right. We all make mistakes, in fact, I made some real blunders in my time, but it's how you react to them, learn from them, and move on, that counts.

So, I hope you enjoy reading this book, and taking a phrase from my passion, rugby, when the time comes for you to kick a 'winning drop goal' I want you to be ready to score those management points and fill you with confidence like any World Cup-winning team!

CHAPTER 1

Kicking It Out of the Park

My version of a winning drop goal

I'M TRACY-ANNE BARKER, not Tracy, Tracey, or Trace; I'm Tracy-Anne, a mentor, coach and trainer.

Like everyone in business, whether employed, self-employed, a business owner, or an entrepreneur, we all have a *back story* – previous life experiences that have influenced and moulded us. And this is mine.

I grew up in a working-class family, on a tough council estate in an industrial blue-collar town. I went to the local comprehensive school and completed an average secondary education. No one from our estate went to university, it wasn't the done thing. We suffered a devastating family loss when my closest brother was killed at the age of 16, I was only 18. It took me over 25 years to deal with the trauma and grief, and only now can I talk about him without crying.

However, every part of my life growing up, at school, and in my early career, was influenced by people who believed in me. Without these people giving me a chance, having faith in my ability, and supporting my progression I would not have developed into the person I am today.

I had, and still do, a strong belief that if you reach for the stars and you work hard your background need not hold you back. If you want to change and you can grasp an opportunity, you can progress.

"It is not how you start, but how you finish"

They say the influence of a good teacher can never be erased and that's so true of those that influenced and believed in me. I can still recall the people who at school helped me so much – Mrs. Marion Fielder-White, my primary teacher, who later was the verger at our wedding (that's a story for another day); Mrs. Fothergill, my first secondary school form teacher; and two influential senior staff – Miss Ayers, the dignified and serene head teacher, and Mrs. Cogley, a warm, if sometimes very strict deputy headteacher.

It was at secondary school where I had my first promotion, as I like to call it. My teachers put their faith in me, and I was given the role of head monitor.

Then in the fifth year, I became deputy head girl. I was thrilled, as this was a significant achievement for this council estate girl! It gave me my first taste of responsibility and helped develop my early communication and public speaking skills that ultimately supported my step up into my first big break in the world of work. My thanks to Mr. Tong the MD, who took me on in an apprenticeship-type role (before there was such a thing) in the world of transport and warehousing. Nowadays it has a much posher sounding name – supply chain & logistics. Mr. Tong believed in my abilities and hired **me,** the only female in a group of five. This set me off for 20 years in a sector which I developed a passion and love for, and still have to this day.

During the economic crash of 2007/08, when companies downsized and changed, I joined a large, successful out-of-town shopping centre as the commercial manager, responsible for training and coordination. I was in their training and recruitment centre, which had started with a strong ethos of recruiting locally and providing training for local people.

Whilst the shopping centre had continued to be highly successful, it was recognised that the training centre had lost its way in fulfilling its ethos of recruiting people locally and helping them build foundations for the future. This needed restoring and refocusing, and I was thrilled to take up the challenge.

After spending time and talking to the staff, I realised that they were inexperienced, and had their backstories of people, bosses, and difficult situations. There was one thing they all had in common, a golden thread that joined them all together, that no one believed in them.

Remember me telling you about the people that had given me a chance, had faith in my ability, supported my progression, and believed in me? It was now time to return that **gift of belief.**

And my belief proved positive.

When you support and champion individuals, you help them achieve the right mindset, focus and ambition. I took it as my responsibility to do just that.

Give your team the gift of belief!

My teams soon began to acquire new skills, knowledge and qualifications. They became masters in their roles and went on to great personal and professional achievements. This included my number two, Ben, who went on to step up and run the centre, which he still does to this very day, doing a tremendous and successful job.

The team and I put the recruitment and training centre back on the map again. The shopping centre, Bluewater in Kent, now has a clear and focused approach to employment and training local people.

We achieved and excelled in many areas, along with our partner organisations, including putting thousands of local people into jobs and training, the first Bluewater online job website, and much more. I'm proud of what we achieved at Bluewater and delighted to see that so much of it is still in place and delivering results.

After nearly 30 years in that world, being a supervisor, team leader, manager, and director, training and managing 1000s of people, I'll admit, I can look back and see that I got it disastrously wrong in the early days. However, those experiences enabled me to set a firm foundation from which to lead a team. Helped me learn how to motivate and manage, how to create a team culture, and embrace a safe culture with a safety net for the team, to enable them to be honest and speak up. You can read more about these aspects of management in Chapter 7, Psychological Safety.

These experiences have given me the foundations I've used to create my own business to mentor, support and coach managers.

I was explaining my business model to a trusted client who has also become a friend over the years, Karen. As I was talking, she stopped me and said she wanted to tell me how she saw me ... I was a bit worried about what she might say at first!

Here's what she said:

"I know you're a trainer, a coach, a business owner and have led large teams at a very high level with a lot of responsibility – but first and foremost you are a mentor, you help managers, aspiring leaders, directors and CEOs to find their way. Yes, you use training and coaching techniques, but I for one feel safe and secure working with you, knowing that I have you on hand to guide, support, and mentor me on my journey".

As you can see, it was all positive, and it was the birth of my fame name, 'The Manager's Mentor'.

It's all Tits, Ass and Balls!

What *do* I mean?

Well, if you hadn't guessed, I'm a HUGE rugby fan. That's where the name of the book comes from.

From supporting my husband and his fellow coaches at our local amateur club to working with young people that were on the edge of their communities, at risk of or often in trouble at school or with the authorities.

They have coached, mentored, and supported those young people, helping them to grow into young adults playing a team sport. This has given these young people a sense of personal pride in their ability, taking personal responsibility for their actions, being prepared to work and train hard. Many of them have gone on to be good rugby players and integral members of the family that is the amateur club.

I follow my beloved national team, England, to international games at Twickenham, and these still fill me with excitement and anticipation. I've watched the All Blacks being beaten by England in a game I remember hubby saying I would never witness!

Witnessing proudly, my 14-year-old stepson singing in the stadium 'Scrum Bar' in front of 100s of fans! And watched the game on TV when we won in Australia in 2003.

From the Barbarians to the Lions, Six Nations to Internationals I, and we as a family, **NEVER** miss a game. One day, we **WILL** get to see our team live, in another World Cup final.

There is a reason for sharing my love of rugby with you. People used to abbreviate my name to TAB, and my closest friends still do! In my younger days, I thought they were being rude and referring to **Tits**, I have some, we all do!, **Ass**, because I usually end up on mine, and **Balls** because of my passion for rugby. I don't play, although I tried really hard to play it at school, but I was shocking! Apparently, people weren't being rude, it was just my interpretation! But it got me thinking ...

Business can be a bit like rugby, running around on the pitch trying to be every player, playing every move, days when you feel like you're the only one on your team getting muddy ... It can be exhausting and sometimes we drop the ball.

I want to help people avoid making an **A**ss out of things, dropping that **B**all, and stopping it all going **T**its up! My aim is to help kick that **B**all out of the park, increase team performance, increase productivity, support your ability to accelerate, and make more money!

And this is my reason for writing this book.

CHAPTER 2

The Cs of Communication

Conversations, conflict, and constructive feedback

I'M GOING TO start by looking at communication, as it's such an important element of management, so this chapter's a big one.

I'll be giving you my Tracy-Anne's Top Tips (TATTs) on how to show you are really listening and understanding your team. There's a quick fun quiz to find out what type of manager you are when it comes to dealing with constructive feedback and TATTs on how to become a master at it.

This is followed by TATTs on how to deal with difficult conversations, and conflict management steps, so you can step into dealing with conflict like a pro.

So how are you going to increase team performance, productivity and make more money?

To coin a rugby phrase, **'It's all about the team'**, and **how** you communicate with your team, an essential foundation for your management skills. Communication seems so simple, yet we can get it so wrong. It can be the biggest cause of upset, mistrust and anxiety in the workplace. When done right, it can improve employee engagement, retention, KPIs, productivity, performance and makes a happier workforce all around. Oh, AND it will make you more money too!

Finding the time for your team

As a manager, I know how hard it is sometimes to find the time to be there for your team. With targets to hit and pressure from the senior management team, it can be difficult, I get it, I've been there.

I found that setting time aside for your team members to come and talk to you, really helped. Set time aside on a regular scheduled and planned basis. And most importantly, communicate that availability to your team!

You may want to set up a diary system using a shared calendar, that they can access and book time with you. Or you may choose to offer an open-door policy.

Example: *Send an email to your team or hold a group meeting in the morning and tell them, "Between 11 am and 2 pm is your time, here's how you can book in".*

If you need to be strict on your time, tell them it's in 30- or 40-minute slots. If you have more time, give them more.

Ok, so you've set the time aside, you're with a team member and they're talking at you.

What are you doing?

Are you listening? Or are you thinking about what to have for dinner tonight? When will this meeting end? Wondering what the score will be in the rugby or football at the weekend? Thinking they really need to cut their hair?

To be honest, we've all been there.

Whether it's at work or home, someone's been talking, and you've not heard a word they've said. Or maybe it's happened to you – you've just explained an issue in full detail and the response you get is, "Sorry, what was that?"

How does that make you feel? How do you think your team member feels?

This is a question I regularly ask the managers I train and coach.

I've got some Top Tips on how to show you're really listening, so you can build rapport and maintain relationships. Using these will help you to understand and influence others, successfully manage challenging situations and help you deal with conflict.

Tracy-Anne's Top Tips (TATTs)

1. **You need to really listen.** This should be obvious, when talking, but too much of the time, it doesn't happen! Be interested in what they have to say and *demonstrate* that you are interested. You can do this in a few ways:

   - Ask questions
   - Verbal nods (nodding the head)
   - Verbal affirmations (I see, I understand)
   - Paraphrase/repeat what they have told you – this is great for gaining clarification or understanding of a matter.
   - Summarising what they have told you. Again, a great way of gaining clarification and understanding.

2. **Make notes of what you have talked about.** Remember, this is an informal meeting, catching up with your team chat. So, the note is only really for your purposes, so you can remember what was said and what you can talk about next time.

This is a great way to build relationships, especially if you've not got a great memory! If a team member told you their brother's baby was due any day, or it was their wedding anniversary soon or their gran was poorly, you can ask them about this next time or at any point you see fit. It shows you listened, and you care.

3. **Be empathetic.** Empathy – the dictionary's definition of empathy is 'the ability to share someone else's feelings or experiences by imagining what it would be like to be in that person's situation.' By understanding where the other person is coming from, this will help you to find common ground and handle the conversation accordingly.

It's also important to remember, as a manager you won't just be dealing with work issues, you'll be dealing with personal ones too, some of which will require empathy.

As an example, you might have a team member who is unable to focus on their work because of a problem at home. You may think that the kind thing to do is enable them to work from home until the situation is resolved. However, work may be giving them space and respite from thinking about what might be a painful and challenging situation. Before assuming that someone has made a mistake or has had a bad day it's important to understand that there is a reason for it, no matter how small or seemingly insignificant. Never jump to conclusions without fully understanding the circumstances. So, don't just assume, talk to them and ask them which approach **they** would prefer.

4. **Know your team and each person.** Not everyone is the same, and each person will be motivated by something different. It's your job as their manager to find out what this is; this can also help when delegating tasks or providing feedback. We explore motivation a little more in Chapter 4.

5. **Provide constructive feedback regularly.** Let your team know what is working and the areas they need to focus on to improve – be honest but not destructive.

   I'll go into giving feedback in more detail in the next section.

6. **Be crystal clear with your team.** Set clear expectations on how you want the job to be done. You want them to be as effective as possible, so make sure you are clear on what you need them to do.

7. **Use the same language.** If they understand what you are saying it's easier for them to be clear on the goals they need to achieve and then work collectively towards them. Use language that is familiar to them. If your industry uses jargon or abbreviations, ensure that you provide crib sheets and training so that they can learn these.

8. **Be proactive in your communication.** Don't wait for the team to come to you and ask questions. Try and pre-empt questions and go out and ask them how they are doing, and how they are feeling.

9. **Keep communication positive.** If someone does a good job, tell them. Positive reinforcement when things go well can help team performance to improve and continue to improve. Saying thank you for a job well done can go a long way.

10. **Use people's names.** People like to hear their names said out loud, it aids communication and promotes a positive culture.

"Bringing out the best in each other"

Being a good leader is about building trust with your team, and having sound relationships with your team will make your job as a manager much easier.

Constructive feedback

Giving feedback, does it make you want to run for the touchline, or are you a 'knee-deep in the scrum, getting down and dirty with the detail' kind of manager?!

Or to bring it back to business, what's your type?

Type A – I don't like giving it, but I'll do it if I really have to.

Type B – I love doing it, I always give feedback but for some reason, people always take it the wrong way.

Type C – I give feedback but I'm not completely confident, so I find I don't always get to the heart of it and the same thing keeps happening.

Type D – I avoid it altogether and just add notes to their files or tell them in their next review, for some reason they don't seem to like this.

Type E – I bury my head in the sand, sweep the problems under the carpet, spend weeks or months ignoring it and then when it explodes wonder what I did wrong – it must be them surely?

Type F – I'm happy to give constructive feedback, it's received really well, and I very rarely have to repeat it.

Wouldn't it be great if we were natural-born **Type F** Managers?!

"We don't practise until we can get it right. We practise until we can't get it wrong."

Just as rugby players practise and develop rugby skills throughout their careers, so to must managers. The more we practise, the more confident we become until eventually, we become natural Type F Managers.

It's time for TATTs

1. **Establish trust.** When you step into your management role, at some point, you will need to give constructive feedback to your team. Therefore, you need to establish an open, trusting relationship and ensure that your team knows that you believe in their potential and appreciate them. Having this trust will help set the tone of future conversations and help you deliver the feedback, and help your team accept it and put any changes in place with little or no resistance. You can use the TATTs from earlier in this chapter to help you establish that trust.

2. **Be timely.** You know what it's like when someone asks you on a Monday what you did at the weekend, and you can't remember? Imagine delivering feedback to someone three weeks after the event. Will they remember why they did it? Will they be able to give any extenuating circumstances? Probably not, as it was so long ago. This is why you need to be timely with feedback. Don't wait days or weeks, you want it to be fresh in both your minds so the conversation will be relevant and actionable. You will find it easier and so will they.

3. **Feedback sandwich.** This is one of my favourites. Start with a positive, something that is a strength, then move on to an area to develop and finish with a strength or positive.

   For example: *I really liked how you handled the client on the phone today, you were calm and professional. Next time, try to avoid using abbreviations as the client may not understand what they are. And the notes you added to the file were really clear and concise, well done.*

Yes, I know not every member of the team or situation is ALWAYS suitable for a feedback sandwich. Sometimes things can be horrendously difficult and saying something positive might mean it will come back and bite you at some stage. Read on to see other tips which can help in such situations.

4. **Focus on the situation, not the person.** If you make it personal, the other person is likely to become defensive and not hear you or become aggressive or upset.

For example: Instead of saying, "You made the files messy" try saying, "The files are messy." Don't make personal attacks.

5. **Be specific not vague.** Drill down to the area for development. As an example, don't say "improve your communication", be specific and pinpoint whether it is written email communication or face-to-face, or perhaps non-verbal such as body language.

For example: *"In this email that was sent out to the customer, there are a lot of spelling mistakes, which doesn't look very professional in our business. Please use spellcheck going forward."*

6. **Concentrate on actionable areas for development.** "I don't like XYZ..." is not useful. If you are talking about non-verbal communication maybe the person crosses their arms when talking to people.

For example: *"When we had the team meeting last week, did you sense a change when we were discussing XYZ, that because this was a difficult subject some of us, including me, crossed our arms. What did you think?"*

7. **Give ideas on how to improve.** Support the person with factual solutions and actions that they can take.

   Example: *"When you have a lot on your task list, create a daily schedule of the top three or four in order of priority that you need to focus on. Stick to the tasks until they are complete, and only then move on to anything that is non-urgent."*

8. **Don't make rash assumptions.** Assumptions that are wrong make you look unprofessional and do not reflect well on you as a manager.

   If we use the Example from Tip 3 – *In this email that we sent out to the customer, you can see there are a lot of spelling mistakes, which don't look very professional in our business. Please can you use spell check going forward?*

   Could there be another reason why there were so many spelling mistakes? Are they dyslexic, and so do you need to provide support to help them? Do they have personal issues that are preventing them from being able to focus and check their work?

9. **Talk things through.** If you can, do this face-to-face or over a virtual platform with the cameras on. There's nothing worse than an email, phone call or message being misinterpreted – it is all too easy for that to

happen and is then very hard to undo. Your vocal tone, body language and emotional inflection such as humour or concern can and will be missing from email, messages and phone calls. So, where you can, meet face-to-face.

10. **Be open and transparent.** If you are not confident in delivering feedback, you may have a tendency to dilute the feedback, talk around it so much that the message isn't clear, and the person leaves the room more confused than when they entered it. You may even be tempted to avoid saying the key thing you needed to say altogether. This is not helping anyone. Preparing for the meeting beforehand with all your key points, and being open and transparent, will ensure your message is delivered clearly with no room for misunderstanding or confusion.

As a manager, it's important that you support your team and gain regular feedback from them. Give them constructive and developmental feedback and work together on areas for development. Don't just criticise them.

Handling difficult workplace conversations

Handling difficult conversations is up there with handling conflict and giving feedback (if the feedback is constructive) – we don't like doing it!

But from time to time as a manager, you'll need to. If you don't, it can lead to further problems especially if the original reason for the difficult conversation is not addressed.

Our instinct is to avoid the intensity and the emotion of a difficult conversation and, you'll be pleased to hear, this is quite normal. Fear of reactions, vulnerability, or even a loss of control for both the manager and individual are reasonable worries.

But, if you adopt the right approach, prepare carefully and have the right skills, mindset and behaviour, you'll be able to handle the conversation and guide it to a successful conclusion that both parties will feel comfortable with.

My best piece of advice for difficult conversations – **don't delay taking action.**

If you delay, in the hope that the issue will be resolved, resolve itself or go away, it's highly unlikely to lead to a positive outcome. Ignoring the issues can lead to the original issue becoming more difficult to resolve.

By tackling problems at an early stage, it may help to resolve the issues, and this then prevents an escalation and breakdown of workplace colleague relationships.

I remember, in one of my roles, I took on an established team where the previous line manager hadn't addressed attendance and productivity issues with a member of staff. There was a culture of putting up with poor performance. This had also created a climate of mistrust amongst the wider team. Taking my Top 10 TATTs for handling difficult conversation, which I'll share with you, I managed the individual, identified the issues they were having, and the poor performance was rectified. The mistrust amongst the team, however, took a long time to resolve.

So, do you see how delaying difficult conversations can lead to demotivated employees, can cost the business lost income or additional expenditure, lead to poor productivity, result in dissatisfied customers, damage of reputation, and can impact staff retention?

Difficult conversations can arise for many reasons, such as:

- poor performance issues
- unacceptable workplace behaviour such as bullying
- providing development feedback
- dealing with sensitive personal employee issues
- turning down holiday or leave requests
- dealing with potential redundancy announcements
- handling disciplinary issues

But you'll be relieved to know, I can help you to make them easier, so as promised here are my top 10 TATTs.

Top 10 TATTs for handling difficult conversations

1. **Be clear** on the purpose of the conversation, avoid anything that is not fact.

2. Adopt the right approach and **plan the conversation**.

3. Provide the staff member with **an opportunity for preparation**.

4. **Recognise your emotional state** and have strategies in place.

5. **Challenge any assumptions or beliefs** you may have, avoid anything that is not fact and cannot be proven.

6. **Open the conversation**.

7. **Present** your side of the conversation.

8. **Listen** to the staff member's explanation, listen actively, and avoid interruption.

9. **Handle your reactions** carefully, be mindful of the staff member's reactions.

10. Find the middle ground and **reach an agreeable solution**.

Are you ready to rise up and take on that difficult conversation like a team captain?!

Conflict

We've handled difficult conversations, looked at different types, and I have shared with you my own personal experience of how I handled one, and given you my TATTs.

It's now time to talk about the elephant in the room, **conflict**.

Conflict management can be one of the most difficult elements of a manager's job. A high percentage of managers I have worked with and train, do not like dealing with conflict – however, it is a necessary and vital aspect of a manager's job.

Conflict management is the process of limiting the negative parts of conflict and increasing the positive aspects.

Why is conflict management important?

Ok, I've got a rugby analogy for you:

This is a scrum.

The idea of a scrum is that the forwards work together to push against the opposite team to get the ball. Now, imagine if one of those teammates has been causing issues in training in the lead-up to the game but the coach has let the behaviour slide, as he didn't want to deal with it.

How do you think the rest of the team will feel? Do you think they'll all be pushing in one direction?

Probably not.

This is in fact an extreme example, as rugby is a highly disciplined sport, and so the forwards not all working together in the scrum is unlikely to happen. One of the great things about rugby and the Rugby Football Union (RFU) is the emphasis on the values of **teamwork, respect, enjoyment, discipline** and **sportsmanship**. But hopefully, you understand the analogy.

Unresolved conflict

If conflict goes unresolved it can foster negative tension, which can lead to poor morale and attendance, and productivity issues. And if the problems continue to go unresolved it can affect employee retention and longer-term cultural issues such as losing the confidence and respect of your team.

It's vital to deal with conflict as early as possible.

How you manage conflict can be a great opportunity for you to solve issues, boost morale and gain the respect of your team.

A common misconception is that it is emotionally sensitive or emotionally intelligent people that are the best at handling these situations. However, emotional intelligence doesn't mean you'll automatically be great at handling conflict in the workplace.

As with all communication skills, conflict management skills must be learned, practised and honed by all managers.

So, here are some practical steps and TATTs to help you improve your conflict management skills.

Conflict management steps

1. **Be aware** of any early signs of conflict
2. **Take a considered** and rational approach
3. **Stay calm** and have strategies in place to help you

4. **Investigate** and take time to find out what has happened
5. **Decide how to tackle the conflict**, decide what is appropriate
6. **Let everyone speak**, if you can get people together
7. **Identify options** and agree on a way forward
8. **Implement the agreed actions**, with everyone taking personal responsibility
9. **Evaluate the outcome** and do not assume that the issue has been resolved
10. **Consider strategies for prevention,** to ensure it doesn't arise again

TATTs of aspects to avoid

1. Ignoring the signs of conflict growing among your team members.

2. Jumping to conclusions about the source of conflict before you investigate it thoroughly.

3. Jumping into the situation too early or pre-empting discussions and imposing your own solution.

   As a manager, it's important that you support your team and gain regular feedback from them. Give them constructive and developmental feedback and work together on areas for development. Don't just criticise them.

Tracy-Anne's Toolkit Takeaway

If you want to make sure you're being crystal clear in your communication, check out my communication checklist for managers.

You can use this as a reminder throughout your day or, if you have some big news to deliver, go through the list and make sure you're delivering it in a way that suits your team's needs.

Communication checklist

- [ ] Set time aside for your team
- [ ] Listen. Really listen.
- [ ] Make notes of the discussion
- [ ] Be empathetic
- [ ] Know your team and each individual person
- [ ] Set clear expectations
- [ ] Adjust your language (avoid jargon and abbreviations)
- [ ] Be curious, ask questions of your team, how are they doing?
- [ ] Make it personal – use your team's names

Constructive feedback

- [ ] Decide which type of manager you want to be
- [ ] Assuming you've said Type F, follow my TATTs on page 29
- [ ] Be open and transparent. Don't assume.

- ☐ Support your individual team members, gain regular feedback from them, and provide developmental and constructive feedback to them.

Difficult conversations

- ☐ Deal with the issue as early as possible
- ☐ Prepare for the conversation and follow my TATTs on page 34
- ☐ Support your team, gain regular feedback from them, and provide developmental & constructive feedback to them.
- ☐ Continue building positive relationships with your team (see page 22 on how to do this) as this will make handling difficult conversations easier.

Conflict management

- ☐ Engage and listen to your team regularly, this will help you to spot signs of conflict early on.
- ☐ Deal with conflict as soon as you see it
- ☐ Use the Conflict Management steps I've provided on page 38
- ☐ Support your team, gain regular feedback from them, and provide developmental and constructive feedback to them.

HOW NOT TO BALLS IT UP | TRACY-ANNE BARKER

CHAPTER 3

Attitude Is Everything

Give yourself the gift of confidence

IN THIS CHAPTER, I'll be sharing with you my TATTs on how to become a confident manager, whilst exploring Imposter Syndrome, what it is, how to combat it, and reminding you it happens to the best of us, including Ollie Phillips who was voted the Best Overseas Rugby Player in France in 2011.

I believe our confidence is precious and personal to us. When you have confidence about a particular task, activity or action it enables us to take steps forward, leaving behind any fear of failure. It's not surprising that **confidence** is one of the most requested training subjects alongside **motivation** which is coming up later in the next chapter.

Confidence is one of the important aspects of a successful career. If you can develop a high level of confidence, have a positive mindset, it will have a positive impact on your emotions and motivation, and your ability to communicate. All in all, impacting positively on your results.

If you have confidence and display confidence it will spread among other people and in turn, they will start to have confidence in you.

Confidence can be 'learned'. However, confidence is not a static skill or state of mind. It fluctuates – some days you are feeling totally in control and fully believe in your abilities, and then on other days you are full of doubts and hesitant about taking decisions. This is normal!

Some people use the phrase 'fake it until you make it'. To be honest, in the past that has gone through my mind before walking onto a stage to give a speech, talking to an auditorium full of people.

But in reality, you do need some experience and expertise relating to your role – you really can't just fake it without a base level of knowledge. And then are you REALLY 'faking it'? You may be less experienced than others, but assuming you have done your research, discussed the topic or activity with others, you are still knowledgeable. Maybe the knowledge is still growing but essentially you are not faking it. So, I reckon we should rephrase this to:

"Go on ... I've got this"

I for one know that this is something that has worked for me in the past.

TATTs to build your confidence

1. **Concentrate on positive thoughts.** Pay attention to what you're thinking. Yes, we cannot ignore the developmental areas we all have, the challenges we have encountered, but focus principally on the positive.

2. **Build a bank of evidence:** a book, a journal, a positivity box, or some place you can record your achievements and the compliments you have received from others.

3. **Identify the things you are most proud of** and what this feels like for you.

4. **Create a list of talents and skills,** along with the impact you have on others.

5. **Manage those negative thoughts:** most of us, me included, have a voice in our heads that tell us to be careful, stopping us from doing things and making progress. My friend Sarah recounts her challenge with voices in her head saying *"If you do this you will make yourself look stupid, you will make a mistake, or they will laugh at you"*. If this happens to you, try and ask yourself, *"What is the worst that can happen if I do this?"* Or *"How likely is it that it will happen?"* If you are prepared and you are as ready at this point as you are ever likely to be, then in most cases you will find that the good outcomes outweigh any of the negatives. Or at least your evaluation will help you prepare, and you will be ready next time!

6. **Seek constructive feedback** from a coach, mentor, or trusted friend. This is an important aspect in building your confidence and gives you evidence for your confidence bank.

7. **Watch and emulate speakers** that exude confidence. Identify what works with their tone of voice, study the pace of the presentation of the talk they are giving. You may want to consider joining a public speaking group to practise in a safe environment or watch presentations online such as TED Talks as they attract great, confident speakers.

8. **Look confident:** I am not suggesting the 'fake it' mantra! Build confidence on the outside, as how you appear to others supports your internal confidence which lessens

the noise of Imposter Syndrome (I.S.), which you can read about in the following pages. Dress neatly and appropriately; you might have a colour that makes you feel instantly brighter and confident, or a tie or shoes, it might even be a scarf. If you feel good wearing it, this will boost your confidence too.

9. **Remember to breathe!** Avoid shallow breaths when nervous as it can make you raise the pitch of your voice and then you appear less confident.

10. And finally, **maintain a good upright posture** – shoulders down and relaxed. When you're sat down it's OK to sit comfortably but don't slouch and avoid closed body language such as folded arms.

If we truly believe we are faking it, that could feed our Imposter Syndrome, or I.S. as it can be known. The word 'fake' is quite negative and so will play into the negativity of I.S. – *"I am not good enough"*, *"I am going to get found out"*, *"I am not as clever, smart, or bright as the others"* and much more.

At this point, I'd love to share an example that an aspiring manager and rugby captain shared with me recently:

When I've done talks or prepped the team before a game the biggest thing that holds us back is the perception we think others have of us. In 99% of cases, people aren't thinking what we believe they are. But still, we let these self-fabricated, negative thoughts infiltrate our minds. It's about letting go of preconceptions and realising that whatever you're thinking is not being thought by others. In most cases, they have a very neutral opinion of you, especially if it's a new group. I always go into a talk now thinking three things:

1. *I know what I'm talking about is important and worthy of people listening.*
2. *The people here are likely here voluntarily, so they want to hear what I have to say. Only a small percentage are uninterested or judging, but that shouldn't matter.*
3. *If I don't do this talk with full confidence, I'm holding myself back. It's uncomfortable because it's abnormal, but until you seek discomfort it will remain unusual, and you won't overcome that barrier. We only truly grow and master things when we are out of our comfort zones.*

Nobody wants to feed the Imposter Syndrome monster, and let's call the rugby captain 'Jacko', and he is completely right – if we stay in the safety zone of comfort, it is really difficult to make progress. Growing and mastery really come when we stretch ourselves outside of our comfort zone.

So, let's take a look at how we can handle and manage I.S.

What is Imposter Syndrome?

We experience a feeling of inadequacy regarding our self-worth and question whether we're qualified enough to achieve something when we're pushed outside our comfort zone. Or, if we don't feel comfortable about a situation, and as a result, our emotions are heightened.

For some of us, this can be a recurring feeling despite repeated external evidence of competence.

This fear or feeling was coined Imposter Syndrome (I.S.) in 1978 by clinical psychologists Pauline Rose Clance and Suzanne A. Imes. I.S. is a persistent fear of being exposed as a fraud or fake, with an inability to internalise our accomplishments and achievements.

It has happened to me.

I had these feelings every time I presented to my senior manager colleagues.

Despite being the subject matter expert, with more relevant experience and knowledge than they had on the topic, I felt unqualified, small, and unsure of my subject matter knowledge because of their depth of experience, even though all their knowledge was in a very different part of the sector.

At no stage did any of my colleagues indicate my knowledge was not good enough, but I still thought I needed to work harder, faster, more hours, and prove myself. Reflecting now, I know that I had excellent knowledge of my field, managed my team, myself and my work to a very high standard and I was always able to do the right thing, take the right action when it was needed, where others did not. And yet, in spite of all this rational, logical evidence that I was not an imposter, I struggled.

I am not the only one who has struggled and still sometimes struggle with I.S. All over the world normal people like you and me, superstars, celebrities and many more have experienced I.S. Many 'high' achievers often doubt themselves, or believe they are not worthy of recognition they may receive.

Take Ollie Phillips, who played in three Heineken Cups, a European Cup Final, and was voted Best Overseas Player in France in 2011. He has said, "*I was a rugby hero and a record-breaker, but I still suffered from imposter syndrome.*"

We probably all know someone who experiences I.S., just as we all work with people who are guilty of the opposite problem, having an over-inflated opinion of themselves. In dealing with I.S. it's important to remember, it does not only affect women, but I have found that many more women recognise it and talk about it. However, I.S. can affect us all.

So how do we find a happy medium, to avoid the arrogance that comes with an over-inflated ego, and lessen the impact that I.S. may have on us?

Here are TATTs that have helped me with I.S. over the last 20 years

1. **Recognise the feelings.** Awareness is key to bringing change in the way you think and act. When you know and say what it is, you open up the possibilities of handling it.

2. **Share it.** Share your concerns, speak to your mentor, coach or trusted colleague who has conquered it effectively.

3. **Review your perception.** It's OK to be wrong, to fail or to not know everything. Just because you do not know something does not mean you are fake or not deserving. Remind yourself that as you progress you will learn more. High-performing teams sometimes lose, miss the goal, targets or achievement. Ask yourself, *"What is the worst that can happen?"* This will help mitigate the fear. Reframe the 'failure' as a learning opportunity. The fact that you will be trying makes your effort admirable, and not a fake.

4. **Affirm and continue to reaffirm your self-worth.** Do not dismiss compliments by attributing your success to external factors. Own it! When you feel undeserving, review previous achievements and positive feedback. Recount the people to who you made a difference. This will assure you that you belong. Do not be ostentatious, that is not a good trait – however, downplaying your success helps no one.

5. **Avoid comparisons.** These can be lethal. Thinking that there are people out there doing similar work to you even better than you, so why should you bother, is not a justified comparison. Do not measure others' highs against your lows. Every successful person was in your place once. It may appear that some people achieve success effortlessly. The reality is that we do not know what struggles another person may be going through.

6. **Learn to value your own strengths and potential.** You will soon realise you have a lot to offer the world.

7. **Evaluate the context.** Reflect on the other times you have felt less confident. Ask yourself if you *always* feel insecure, uncertain and unconfident. This will help you identify when you did feel in control and the steps you took. Maybe you could use the same techniques and strategies again. Write some notes in a journal or notebook so that you can remember those feelings, and how to get back to an increased positive mindset again.

8. **Pursue your goals.** I have found the best way to challenge I.S. is to continue taking action – do not allow yourself to be overwhelmed by how you feel. It takes a lot of courage to persist in challenging situations, recognising your feelings, the steps you can take, and evaluate the context in which you can achieve. None of us know how much we can accomplish until we try. The world needs action-takers, innovators and leaders to look up to, so be proud of your achievements, ability, and aspirations.

9. **Self-coaching.** What can you do to help yourself? How can you encourage yourself to overcome I.S.? Positive mantras such as, *"I've got this"* can work, as can positive affirmations such as, *"I am a respected manager, I am an expert in my field, I am * * * ..."*, fill in the blanks. This type of positive self-talk can help you to alter your subconscious thoughts, and re-wire the negative thought patterns to positive ones. Not only that but you'll begin to act in line with this positive self-talk and will eventually become that person.

10. **MOST of all, be proud of YOU!** Imposter syndrome can be a **BITCH**. But with a little work each day, remember that 99% of people will not be thinking what we may

believe they are. Don't let your self-beliefs and negative thoughts find their way into your mind. What you have to say *does* have value and it *is* worth others listening to what you say. Don't focus on the very small percentage that may be less interested. Practise these each day and you'll soon leave I.S. for dust as you gain confidence, sprinting up the pitch ready to score that rugby try as you accelerate in your role.

Checklist: Quick steps to feeling confident:

- ☐ Collect evidence of your own achievements
- ☐ Collate a list of your skills and talents
- ☐ Create a new mantra. Try "Go on ... I've got this!"
- ☐ Emulate your favourite speakers
- ☐ Dress neatly, unfold arms, upright posture, shoulders down and relaxed, and BREATHE!

Imposter Syndrome – points to remember

- It can affect us all
- Recognise the feelings and share them with a mentor, coach or trusted colleague

- Reframe any thoughts of failure as learning opportunities
- Own the compliments!
- Avoid comparisons
- Value your strengths and potential
- Think of a time you felt in control and the steps you took; repeat them
- Continue taking action

CHAPTER 4

Becoming a Motivation Maestro

The importance of motivating your team

AS A MANAGER, you need to understand **what** motivates each individual. You are managing a team of individuals, all with different personalities, which equal different motivators. And it's down to you as their manager to find out what that is. Hint: it's not always about the money. I'm going to tell you how to uncover your team's motivators, what happens if you don't do this, and ways you can improve motivation.

Did you know that according to *Inc.com* over 60% of staff leave an organisation because of their manager? That's why it's so important for managers to upskill, gain support, and create opportunities for the team to develop their skills.

Every day, all of us make decisions on how much effort to put into our work. Our team is no different and, as managers, we have the perfect opportunity to influence those decisions and motivate the team. However, first, we must know what actually motivates each member of the team.

Even temps can be motivated and increase productivity

I remember my first summer job, working in a catering team for a local hospital. I was employed for six weeks as a catering assistant. Back in the 1980s, the catering manager had a command-and-control approach which was usual for those times. He was stressed because staff were off sick and we 'temps' were there to fill the gaps. In the first few weeks, he didn't get the best out of us because it was just about following orders and we were not empowered to use our initiative.

Sue, the supervisor, soon stepped in. She took the time to find out a little about us, found out what motivated us, and trained us in other tasks in the team, and soon productivity increased. Not only were we filling the gaps in the kitchen, loading the industrial dishwashers, washing floors, and serving food for patients ready for porters to take to the wards. We were also working in the staff café, responding to last-minute specialist requests from the matrons and helping the chefs with food preparation. We went that extra mile because we were now motivated to do so.

So how can you become a Motivation Maestro?

At times, managers can find it frustrating and difficult to motivate their teams.

Unless you truly understand what motivates people, and position yourself to support and motivate them during periods of change or challenging economic circumstances, you will find it very difficult to aid their motivation.

In all businesses – sole traders, small or medium-sized, large and right up to multi-nationals – everyone involved needs to find their motivation. This vital ingredient helps productivity, increases customer retention and customer growth, helps business evolution, and supports adaptation to external and internal factors that impact the business.

When there is a business crisis, most organisations focus on tactical, operational solutions. They focus on making sure the 'number' of tickets, projects or business activities has been acted upon. This is a blunt "if I can measure it, it must be working" approach.

While some in the team may respond well to this, it is not the way to carry everyone through the process.

That's why it's important to help your team to be adaptable in any changing situation; this will help them to remain productive regardless of whether they are working remotely from home, have returned to the office, work site, factory, production plant, outlet or workspace, or even if they use a co-working space. In this post-Covid world of increasingly hybrid working arrangements, this is more important than ever.

How you do this boils down to your skills as a manager to motivate your team. As I mentioned earlier, it's important to understand the factors that influence their motivation, and the only way to do this is to engage with them on a regular basis by asking questions, striking up genuinely interested conversations, and getting a real understanding of them and what makes them tick.

Maslow's hierarchy of needs built upon a theory of human motivation, and he stated that, "People had five sets of needs, which come in a particular order. As each level of needs is satisfied, the desire to fulfil the next set kicks in." Only at that final stage would they be performing and motivated at their peak.

Maslow's theory has been used to identify staff needs and fulfilment, by delegating projects, creating a change in job title, or a more flexible approach to their working pattern, allowing them time for personal development either in or outside of work.

There are numerous other theories that explain motivation, such as Herzberg's Motivation Hygiene Theory, Vroom's Expectancy Theory and McClelland's Need Theory.

However, as a manager, regardless of any theory you may choose to follow, the fundamental point is that you need to understand your team so that you **CAN** motivate them. The success of your business really does depend on how successfully you can motivate your workforce. I encourage you to look into this topic further and read more about it. It has proved to be a popular one in the training that I deliver for organisations and individuals.

The impact of poor motivation on your team

Ask yourself the question, how bad can it actually be if my team isn't motivated?

I like to approach this by linking it to a sports team, and the example I choose is the England Rugby Team. If they were unmotivated, do you think they'd try their best and stand a chance of winning the game?

Almost certainly not.

The same is true for your team, and the effects of an unmotivated team can be far-reaching:

- loss of income
- reduced profits

- loss of clients
- sickness and absence among the team
- difficulty recruiting new staff and increased costs
- increased stress levels among the managers, business owners and staff
- increased client complaints and damage to business reputation

In other words, motivation affects the quality of every aspect of your business!

So, including a strategy for motivating the business and the team within it is vital for business success. Having a well thought out motivational strategy will be key to helping your business performance thrive. Fail to include this and ultimately the business will fail. It's as stark as that!

Be prepared, implement your motivation strategy to underpin your success. Become a Motivation Maestro!

TATTs for creating a motivated team

1. **Offer non-monetary incentives.** A simple verbal thank you, said with feeling and meaning, a handwritten letter or card, free or subsidized food or drinks, a reward or recognition scheme.

2. **Build and maintain positive relationships with colleagues.** Negative relationships significantly impact on the mood and experience in the workplace.

3. **Build and maintain positive relationships with managers and business owners.** It's important to create and sustain effective communication, as this will help to build up the two-sided trust and rapport that every business needs. This will help you to communicate a clear direction, so you'll be able to support and motivate the team.

4. **Create a clear company culture.** A lack of belief or understanding about the organisation's goals leads to a negative attitude, lower commitment, and low job satisfaction. Ensure you share the goals with your team and that they understand them.

5. **Offer learning opportunities.** Many employees naturally want to do a good job to help them feel they are achieving. Temporary staff want to acquire new skills for personal development. Millennials and Generation Z highlight learning opportunities as something key for them. Create opportunities for all team members to attend courses, experience on-the-job training or job shadowing.

6. **Ensure work is engaging.** No matter what the task, job role or topic if you want your teams to be motivated in their work, it's important you make their work engaging, interesting, varied and challenging.

7. **Develop clear organisational processes.** While processes on their own are not motivational tools, they are closely linked to areas that impact staff desire, enthusiasm and willingness to work. Efficient, clear processes are vital to stimulate and retain the team.

8. **Create a clear work-life balance.** Everyone needs this, but it is up to managers to set the right example and to ensure that the expectations of working hours are known by all. The days of a long-hours culture being acceptable and motivating are long-gone.

9. **Empower your team.** One of the ways to do this is to give your team the opportunity to experiment to solve a problem that matters to your business. Identify something which has been a difficult problem to solve, one where seeing things from a different angle is likely to unearth some solutions. For example, ask, "What additional useful service can we give our customers?" or "What process or business system is broken and how can we fix it?" Give the team the time and the authority to collaborate and support each other to find and implement solutions.

10. **Provide meaningful work.** For permanent staff this means ensuring that they can make a difference in their role. They need to see how they tangibly contribute towards the wider goals of the business and indeed of society. I have mentioned Millennials and Gen Z employees. Research shows that for this intake, 'making a difference' is an extremely important motivator in their lives, and you need to tap into this instinct in a genuine way. In a charity setting, it is important that volunteers understand the goals and the mission that you have. For temporary staff, make this effort too, ensuring they know that what they do plays an important part in the wider picture.

"Dedication + Motivation = Success"

Motivation checklist

So, you've got my tips, you understand how a demotivated team can damage a business's overall performance, so here's a checklist to make sure you're not missing anything.

To be a Motivation Maestro, ask yourself, am I:

- ☐ Clear on each of the individual motivators for my team?
- ☐ Giving constructive feedback and providing performance improvements?
- ☐ Setting clear goals with opportunity to reward success?
- ☐ Offering personalising rewards relevant to each individual?
- ☐ Re-designing or making changes to job roles to increase individual's motivation?
- ☐ Offering learning and development opportunities?
- ☐ Creating a suitable work/life balance?
- ☐ Empowering my team to achieve, or do I put barriers in the way?
- ☐ Re-enforcing positive behaviour and successful achievements?
- ☐ Creating a clear purpose and meaning to the work and to people's roles?

Tracy-Anne's Motivational Games

It can be difficult to keep your team focused and motivated, so why not try these fun games, which are proven to work!

You will see that there are different formats of them, to allow them to be played in-the-room or virtually, so that you involve your remote workers too.

A Pat on the Back Game – in-the room

Step one – Line up your team.

Step two – Tell them to pat each other on the back and mention a positive reason why you're giving them a pat on the back.

This can be mentally rewarding for your team and will promote positive vibes.

If you want to, add a reward incentive and the team member with the most pats receives a small reward. If appropriate, you can join in too, gain a pat on the back or give out pats on the back.

A Pat on the Back Game – virtual

Step one – Give your team an order in which to go, or number each member 1- X, depending on however many team members you have.

Step two – Tell them to mention a positive reason to the next person in order, why they're giving them a pat on the back.

If you want to add a reward or incentive, you could send an e-voucher or send something in the post.

Decorate your Space or Office game – in-the-room

You might like to do this to celebrate a festival such as Diwali, Easter, Maghi, Eid etc.

This type of content works well because naturally people are competitive and will strive to create the best possible space.

And an area that looks better can lead to increased productivity.

Decorate your Space or Office Game – virtual

The ethos is the same, but you encourage people to create the most vivid and attractive virtual background space, relevant to the theme.

The Drawing Game – in-the-room

A team game that encourages communication and most importantly listening. It is deceptively simple but effective.

Step one – Two players sit back-to-back, and one team member will hold a picture containing an object or words.

Step two – The person holding the picture then describes what they see without using a direct word that may give a hint to what it is.

Step three – The other person holding pen and paper draws the object according to what can be deduced from the verbal description and interpretation.

The result is always fun to see, and you can give it a try too.

The Drawing Game – virtual

This takes a small amount of preparation.

Step one – The day before the game, ask each team member to look for a picture containing an object or words.

Step two – On the day, each person takes turns to describe their picture whilst all the other team members draw what they think it is.

The team member with the greatest likeness to the picture wins that round.

After each person has been, whoever has the most wins from each round, wins overall.

Fun games can work well for motivating your team. Rewarding positive results and positive behaviour with a prize or another incentive can be a real winner.

The result is a motivation boost for your team which results in greater productivity and better work from your team members.

Motivation is dynamic and changes over time. It's a manager's responsibility to identify and react to those changes because understanding what your employees want to achieve as individuals and showing them how to do it is one of the main principles that will help you to build a strong and engaged team.

HOW NOT TO BALLS IT UP | TRACY-ANNE BARKER

CHAPTER 5

The Good, the Bad and the Ugly

Good relationships = enjoyable work

GONE ARE THE days when being a manager meant sitting in a big chair, overseeing your team, and giving orders. That may have worked in the '80s but not anymore. Nowadays, you need to focus on building relationships with your team. That means getting out of yourself and into the team. And remember, making connections with your team is positive for your mental health and that of your team.

So, I'm going to help you to understand the additional benefits of building good relationships; how to handle the not-so-great ones and of course, give you my TATTs on how to build relationships.

I talked in Chapter 4 about building relationships with your team for motivational purposes, and understanding what drives them, and in Chapter 2 about dealing with difficult conversations and conflict.

Our desire to feel connected to others is a basic human need that has a significant impact on our mental and physical health.

A significant contributor to workplace stress is psychosocial hazards related to the culture within an organisation, such as poor interpersonal relations and a lack of policies and practices related to respect for workers (Stoewen, 2016).

This is an environment that we spend more time in than almost any other aspect of our lives so it's vital that we have positive relationships in the workplace.

Cultivating good relationships

Humans are naturally social, and we all know that **good** relationships make work more enjoyable. Great work relationships help to increase confidence and develop teamwork. This in turn helps the team embrace change and creates an environment of innovation.

Building and maintaining good working relationships starts with a culture of:

- Building trust
- Encouraging mutual respect
- Developing self-awareness
- Creating a culture of inclusion
- Fostering open and honest communication
- Being mindful in thought and actions

The good, the bad, and the ugly of management relationships

Unfortunately, there are times when you'll have to work with someone you don't get on with. With the rise of virtual workspaces, many colleagues are finding that they are benefiting from some time apart. But even communicating virtually can cause misunderstandings or tension.

Whilst it's natural to avoid people who cause friction, it's not always feasible or for the good of your team. But don't worry, here are a few tactics to mend or maintain a professional relationship.

- **Reflect on your positive history**. If a good relationship has taken a turn for the worse, research shows that reflecting on positive experiences with a co-worker can strengthen a broken bond.
- **Use an impartial mediator.** Setting up and using this resource can help to bridge the divide and help find a quick resolution.
- **Look at yourself.** When we feel negative about someone, we can become impatient, get angry, and demotivate others. Others can direct those negative behaviours back at us.

"Some want it to happen, Some wish it would happen, Others make it happen"

Building close connections with people can take time but if you're willing to put the effort in, it will pay off as you see improvements in productivity and a greater likelihood that you are achieving your targets.

TATTs to help you build better relationships with your colleagues

1. **Identify your relationship needs.** This may sound a little unusual, but do you know what you need from the other person? And do you know what they need from you? Understanding these needs can be instrumental in building better relationships.

2. **Develop your people skills.** Good relationships start with good people skills. These are important for both managers and team members. Some examples that you could develop are putting yourself forward for work social events or situations where you need to interact with new people. If you are not yet a manager, to gain experience in this area, offer to supervise work experience students or interns if your business has an intern programme. It will help you to communicate clearly and concisely and can also improve your negotiation skills.

3. **Focus on your Emotional Intelligence.** Emotional Intelligence (EI) is your ability to recognise your emotions, and better understand what they're telling you. By developing your EI, you'll become more adept at identifying and handling the emotions and needs of others. You will find more about this in Chapter 8.

4. **Practise mindful listening.** People respond better to those who truly listen to what they have to say. By practising mindful listening, hearing what the other person says and by talking less, you can understand more. This will build trust which is essential in relationship building.

5. **Schedule time to build relationships.** You could ask a colleague out for a cup of coffee or give 'one minute of kindness and support' by commenting on a colleague's LinkedIn post you enjoyed reading or a report they have written. These little interactions take time to take effect but lay the groundwork for strong relationships.

6. **Manage your boundaries.** Make time, but not too much! Sometimes, a working relationship can impair productivity, especially when a friend or colleague begins to monopolise your time. It's important to set your boundaries and manage how much time you devote to social interactions at work, so being clear and transparent on this will help.

7. **Appreciate others.** Everyone, from your boss to the apprentice, wants to feel that their work is appreciated. So, genuinely compliment the people around you when they do something well. Give praise and support. Recognising others' efforts and achievements will open the door to great work relationships.

8. **Be positive.** Focus on being positive, as positivity is contagious, and people gravitate to those that make them feel good.

9. **Avoid gossiping.** It's easy to get caught up in office politics or gossip, but beware, as it can ruin workplace relationships. If you're experiencing conflict with someone in your group, talk to them directly about the problem. Gossiping with other colleagues will only exacerbate the situation, accelerating mistrust and animosity.

10. Be open and honest. You must be transparent in your conversations and be open and honest with the other person. Don't lie or tell untruths as these will seriously damage any relationship.

Businesses need laughter. The days of being overly professional and stuffy are mainly long gone. I have heard many stories from friends in the medical profession where their humour in the most difficult and challenging situation has helped get them through. Use it to break tension and bring people together.

Good belly laughs with friends and colleagues can work wonders, as they trigger the release of endorphins, stimulate circulation, and aid relaxation, which may contribute to reducing some physical symptoms of stress. There needs to be boundaries to any humour but 'inside jokes', funny stories etc can really help to build rapport with your team and among your team.

Building your networks internally and externally

Good managers should be able to build networks both internally and externally within a business. A strong performing and functioning team is important to boosting staff morale, performance, and completion of work. The manager must motivate all stakeholders, not just their direct staff. Also, they should support group and team working and be committed to fairness, inclusion and diversity.

Three quick steps to building good relationships

1. Take an assessment of the other person and your position
2. Listen to the other person and understand them
3. Find common ground or a common theme that works for both individuals

It's important to recognise your role within the organisation and how your relationship with the other person could work.

In the construction industry, I experienced first-hand the very best example of relationship building from one of my new team managers. While I have been fortunate to work with many great teams and managers, this individual sticks out as a role model for effective relationship building. From day one she really understood the need to build her network and worked hard at the three steps mentioned above. She garnered huge support and built strong networks internally and externally. She delivered great results and had a highly positive impact on the business during my time as her line manager.

Managers must be able to influence others up and down the organisational hierarchy, and her relationship-building was a brilliant example of this.

The importance of listening: This is a key management skill, especially in relationship building and maintenance. To influence others, it's vital to understand them. To be able to successfully manage challenging situations where there may be conflict. If you can try to see where the other person is coming from and understand them, it will help you to find common ground. Having empathy and an interest in other people helps to build relationships.

Create a code of conduct: A code of conduct, either from a professional membership body or developed from your own values and beliefs, is important. How you treat other people and wish to be treated are useful underpinning factors in how you successfully manage your team, stakeholders and relationships.

If managers have effective relationships, it helps the business to spread knowledge, skills, and the ability to share information. Importantly, they enable staff and managers to ask for help. If relationships are good, it becomes easy to gain advice from a mentor, business colleague or associate – a great method for individuals and businesses to develop and become more productive. As the saying goes, 'Work smarter not harder'. Having good relationships makes that a possibility.

So, let's recap

- Our desire to feel connected to others is a basic human need and impacts on our mental and physical health
- Poor interpersonal relations are a significant contributor to workplace stress
- We spend more time at work than outside of work; so, it's important we have positive relationships in the workplace
- Great work relationships increase confidence and teamwork, and enable teams to embrace change, and create an environment of innovation

Building relationships – your culture checklist

Thinking about your team/company, tick all that apply when you consider how each person builds relationships:

- ☐ We're encouraged to build trust
- ☐ There is mutual respect amongst us
- ☐ We are all self-aware
- ☐ We are inclusive
- ☐ We're open and honest in our communication
- ☐ We are mindful in thought and actions
- ☐ We're encouraged to network internally and externally

If you want to take this a step further, you could ask your team to tick all that they think applies. Compare your responses and work together on any differences.

Tracy-Anne's Building Relationships Games

Here are a couple of games you can play to get your team talking to each other more, helping explore a little more about them, their likes and dislikes.

The Sweet Game – in-the-room

Step one – Divide the team into groups of 4 or 5

Step two – Pass round a bag of sweets, say to everyone to take as many or as few sweets as they would like.

Step three – Go around the group and for every sweet they took, each team member then shares something unique about them that others do not already know. Continue until the sweets have all gone.

N.B. If someone took more than one sweet, they have to share more than one thing about themselves!

For the virtual version, it's re-named
The Number Game

Step one – Divide the team into groups of 4 or 5 and create a breakout room for each group.

Step two – Get everyone to choose a number 1-6 and write it on a piece of paper and hold it up for everyone to see.

Step three – Go around the group and for every number they wrote, each team member shares something unique about them that others do not already know. Continue until all the numbers have been covered.

The Raffle Game – in-the-room

Step one – In advance, prepare questions on pieces of paper, fold each piece and put them in a cup or bowl.

Step two – Taking turns, one person pulls a piece out (like a raffle) for the next person and they have to answer the question.

Some examples you could write:

- What is your favourite place to eat?
- What is your favourite film?
- What is your favourite song?
- Where do you like to go on holiday?
- How many languages can you speak?
- What is your favourite book/author?
- What's a unique thing in your office?
- Did you have a favourite childhood toy, if so, did it have a name?

The Raffle Game – virtual

Step one – In advance prepare questions on pieces of paper, fold each piece, and number each one.

Step two – Tell your team they can choose any number between 1 and X (insert how many are numbered).

Step three – Taking turns, one person calls out a number and then they answer the question.

There are lots of quiz formats on the internet, here is one that I have adapted over the years, using multiple key questions that have been discussed with managers I have worked with.

Building Relationships quiz

This quiz will help you identify areas where you need to improve relationships.

Make a note of your answers, and then at the end add up all the ones where you answered 'Agree'.

1. I enjoy speaking to people, asking them about their weekend:
   ☐ Agree ☐ Disagree ☐ Neutral
2. I enjoy good relationships at work, they make work more fun and enjoyable:
   ☐ Agree ☐ Disagree ☐ Neutral
3. I feel more confident working with people that I like:
   ☐ Agree ☐ Disagree ☐ Neutral
4. Having good relationships with my colleagues helps me cope with the stresses of changing circumstances at work:
   ☐ Agree ☐ Disagree ☐ Neutral
5. When I fall out with people in my team it upsets me and prevents me from being productive
   ☐ Agree ☐ Disagree ☐ Neutral
6. I rarely argue with my colleagues, as I am good at understanding their perspective:
   ☐ Agree ☐ Disagree ☐ Neutral

7. When other team members are not included, I feel uncomfortable:

   ☐ Agree ☐ Disagree ☐ Neutral

8. I find it easy to express myself calmly and with clarity:

   ☐ Agree ☐ Disagree ☐ Neutral

9. I am respectful of individuals' differences even if their quirky ways annoy me:

   ☐ Agree ☐ Disagree ☐ Neutral

Scores

6 or more Agree – well done, you are ace at building work relationships; you are inclusive and considerate of others. It is important that you don't take those strong relationships for granted. Continue to foster a positive working environment.

3 – 5 Agree – there are elements that you succeed in, regarding relationship building. However, you may need to develop your self-awareness knowledge to help you understand yourself and others in your team.

Less than 3 Agree – there is some work to do, so *revisit* this relationship chapter in a few weeks (Chapter 5) and reflect on the areas in which you can develop your skills. Share those with a peer to gain support and accountability to help your progress.

And, if you are looking for a supportive group of managers who will champion and support you, along with online resources to develop your skills, **The Managers' Circle** could be for you. You'll find details on how to join this in the bibliography on page 191.

The power of Thank You – it's a gift that keeps on giving

Generosity is a great tool for building good relationships. Being generous can make a huge difference to productivity and the happiness of your team. It doesn't mean spending lots of money or buying extravagant gifts. It should just be something that is a thread throughout the working year and throughout your day-to-day business life.

A client recently asked for advice on buying gifts as a way of giving staff a treat. They didn't have a large budget but wanted to reward good performance. This led me to reflect on how I have managed this tricky issue when I wanted to provide a Christmas gift for staff, praise staff for a job well done, or generally raise the spirits of the team when times were tough.

Here are some TATTs to show your thanks

1. **Give praise and positive feedback.** Outside of performance management, when done well, this can support performance management improvements. Although it can be hard to praise your team if there is no culture of praise in an organisation, you can change that. So, if you believe your team could have done the job better, choose the parts that they did well and give them some praise. See how they respond, and then foster a culture of analysing what went well and what could be worked on to be better next time. Most people want to

go home at the end of the working day feeling they have done a good day's work, so this will support the drive for motivation and productivity improvements.

2. **Share information.** As managers, we should be supplied with the information we need through our business structure. Many managers moan about silo operations and poor communication. Some managers like the power that information gives them, and of course not all our team need to know every piece of information. So, a willingness to share information and ideas with your team is positive. Don't be afraid that someone in your team may use the information to come up with an idea before you – they are your team, and they want to make you proud. Therefore, fostering a sharing culture will reflect positively on both you and them.

3. **Be generous in sharing projects and tasks.** As managers it may be tempting to give only the rubbish jobs to less senior team members. However, your team succeeding and doing brilliantly with an interesting, high-quality project or task reflects positively on them, the team and you as the manager. So, share the good stuff around!

4. **Offer encouragement and stay positive.** As managers, when under pressure it can be difficult to keep a smile on your face and be positive all the time. Particularly if you have a specific preference for how tasks should be tackled, and the team doesn't match up to your expectations. Yes of course bad work needs to be addressed, including performance management and capability if needed. However, if it's not laziness or

sloppy work leading to any shortcomings, focus instead on guiding your team and encouraging them. Revert to mentoring or coaching them to support improvement.

5. **Create a gratitude wall.** Use a flip chart, bulletin board, or wall near your team. Use Post-it notes or something similar to write who and what you're thankful for. You could even encourage your team to do the same about their teammates.

6. **Give out treats.** This is not for all managers, and some are non-believers. If you are minded to do so, giving out treats does not need to be extravagant. You will be amazed at the effect a small gesture can create. So, maybe monthly at a team meeting, or just at an impromptu moment, bring in a packet of biscuits, a tub of sweets, or some fresh fruit. Alternatively, if you are a keen baker or cook, bake a small cake or cookies.

7. **Hand out gifts.** Some organisations have rules and procedures that discourage this, so it's important to check your organisation's policy. My personal rule is to treat your team all the same and not have favourites, so don't spend more on one team member versus another. That can lead to resentment and hostility. But as with treats, you may be surprised at the disproportionately strong motivational effect a small gift or gesture can have.

8. **Offer an early finish or days off.** Everyone loves an early finish on a Friday or even better, the whole of Friday off! So why not reward someone with either of these? You'll

probably find the rest of the team will be extra motivated if they know there's a chance to get Friday's off.

9. **Give out personalised vouchers.** Again, you need to check your organisation's rules and procedures but saying thank you with a gift voucher for their favourite restaurant or shop shows how much you appreciate them and, as it's for their favourite place, it shows you've been listening to them.

10. **Thank them by letting them be the boss for the day.** Let team members sit in on meetings, give them the use of their own office, a prime parking spot, or any other perks managers at your organisation might have. It'll give them a taste of what it's like to be in charge and will also motivate the rest of the team; who doesn't want to be the boss for the day?

Reflect and be comfortable with your management style

Being a manager requires a certain amount of generosity to keep smiling when times are tough. Reflect on what works for you, and don't just copy other managers because you feel you have to. Be comfortable with your management style, consider some of these tips and be generous to your team. By doing so, productivity and ultimately profitability will improve.

Ways of saying thank you

There is a myriad of templates and ideas on the internet, but here is one that I have used that I have found to be particularly effective – a thank-you email to a team member.

Feel free to change the wording to suit your requirements.

Dear Neil,

I can't tell you how much I appreciated you filling in for me at today's divisional meeting. The group could not afford to lose a week if the project we are planning will be ready for launch next month. The actions are on schedule, which makes our timely preparation even more critical.

I can't believe that toothache was raging this morning when we planned to meet and have this crucial meeting. Thanks to you, we are still on target. I also appreciate the minutes that Elizabeth forwarded to me. It looks like you had a most productive meeting, and the notes have really helped to keep me in the loop.

Once again, thank you Neil, for jumping in at the last minute and doing such a great job.

Best wishes

Tracy-Anne

Explaining their impact and why it was important really helps to communicate the wider impact on the team and organisation and ensures that the thank you is more meaningful.

CHAPTER 6

Decisions, Decisions, Decisions

How to make your own and decisions for others

AS A MANAGER you'll have countless decisions to make throughout your career. Some will be small and have little impact, whereas others could be huge and cost thousands. Not only that but there will also be times when the decision needs to be made quickly, with very little evidence or information to go on.

So how can you improve your decision-making skills as a manager? I say skills because decision-making is a skill and over time it can be improved.

This topic takes little bits of what I've already talked about – communication, confidence, motivation, and sound relationships – plus some things you probably already do and know.

You won't always get it right

First, let me tell you a tough fact – you will make wrong decisions. This doesn't mean you don't know what you're doing or that you're a bad manager. Far from it – in fact, if you feel this way at any time just flip back to Chapter 3 and read my tips on managing Imposter Syndrome.

As Mark Twain said, "Good decisions come from experience, experience comes from making bad decisions".

And it's also worth remembering, we can't always be in control of our decisions. Sometimes as a manager our role is how we execute the results of any decision with honesty, compassion, and build on the trust we have in place with our team.

Types of decision-making

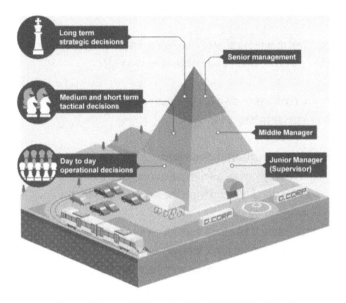

Image: bbc.co.uk/bitesize/guides/zkdc7nb/revision/1

This illustration is a good pictorial representation of the types of decision which need to be made, and who should be making them. Let's look at these types of decision-making.

Operational: These are your day-to-day decisions – things like a member of your team asking for advice on a file they're working on or authorising someone's annual leave.

Tactical: These are medium and short-term decisions such as implementing workflows, apportioning resources, recruiting new employees, developing process improvement etc.

Strategic: These are long-term decisions usually made by senior management. These are ones where you plan a course of action based on long-term goals and vision.

Take a few moments now to consider the decisions that you need to make – are they mainly operational or tactical?

Can you create your own list of examples for each type? Here are a few examples to help you:

Everyday operational decisions
- The projects or tasks require your team members' attention for identifying the key priorities for the day, week, or month
- Deciding if you have enough resources to staff the department in the key busy periods
- Identifying which team members you can delegate tasks to

Tactical decisions:
- Product price changes, either to incorporate additional costs or overheads or respond to a changing market need
- Department changes or re-organisation to respond to a resourcing need, client requirement or business need
- Altering work schedules, such as responsibility for certain key tasks

Strategic decisions:
- Large changes to organisation structure
- Infrastructure investment, such as capital investment
- Investment in new products or services

Where and how decisions are made in business

Depending on where you work or how long you've been there, you may have seen how and where decisions are made.

Thinking about the business you work for, are the decisions mainly:

A. Taken by senior managers and/or the head office.

B. Made by each department; each has authority to make their own decisions.

If you answered A, this means that decisions are centralised, conversely if you answered B, this means they are de-centralised.

Both have their advantages and disadvantages, as you can see here:

Advantages of centralisation	Disadvantages of centralisation
Easier to implement common policies and practices for the business as a whole	More bureaucratic – often extra layers in the hierarchy
Easier to coordinate and control from the centre – e.g., with budgets	Lack of authority down the hierarchy may reduce manager motivation

Quicker decision-making (usually) – easier to show strong leadership	Customer service does not benefit from the flexibility and speed available in local decision-making
Advantages of de-centralisation	**Disadvantages of de-centralisation**
Improve staff motivation	Decision-making may not be strategic
Better level of customer service	Difficult to ensure consistent practice
Decisions are made closer to the customer	Less control and ability to coordinate financial matters etc.

This list is not exhaustive and as you can see both types are needed in business, and each has its benefits.

As a manager, it's important to recognise how decision-making is conducted in your business. If you think it is too centralised, challenge this. After all, that's a role of management – to look for new ways of working and always seeking to improve things.

Where's your mindset at?

We're not all the same and we do not all think the same. Remembering this will help you, especially when it comes to group decision-making.

Taking a look at the two different mindsets below, which one are you?

Mindset A

In a group do you seek to persuade others, defend your position and downplay your weaknesses? And do you view decision-making as a contest?

Mindset B

In a group do you navigate decision-making using collaborative problem-solving and asking questions? And are you open to constructive criticism?

Which one?

Well, which did you choose? And does that mean the other one can't be good or useful when it comes to decision-making?

The names for these two mindsets are **Advocacy** and **Enquiry**. Can you guess which is which?

Mindset A is Advocacy: this refers to stating one's views as you've already seen.

Mindset B is Enquiry: refers to asking questions and working collaboratively.

As you've probably already guessed, there are pros and cons to both.

But, knowing we have different mindsets enables us to build relationships, work collaboratively and understand that Mike from Accounts isn't just being a pain in the ass, that's just his mindset.

Furthermore, studies have found that decisions made by diverse teams deliver 60 percent better results.

As a manager, create an environment within your team where an enquiry mindset is encouraged. Your team will thank you for it, as they're now not only thinking more critically and so feel empowered, but they will also feel their points of view are welcomed and valued rather than discouraged and dismissed. And by doing this, you're preparing them for the next stage of their development, particularly if they want to be the next manager.

And for your personal management skills, make sure you have the right balance between Advocacy and Enquiry. There will be occasions where you will need to persuade others (Advocacy) that your course of action is right. However, providing you have shown your team you are open to a collaborative approach (Enquiry) when it comes to decision making, they won't mind a bit of Advocacy every now and then.

OK, I know that's a lot of information, I mean who knew there was so much behind decision-making?!

A recap on decision-making

- There are three types of decision-making: Operational, Tactical, Strategic.
- Decisions can be made in a centralised or de-centralised way; both have their advantages and disadvantages.
- There are two types of mindsets to consider when managing people and making decisions: Advocacy and Enquiry. It's important to have a balance of both and be aware of your team members' mindsets.

Decision-making preferences

Let's start by looking at the ways in which people make decisions:

Autocratic (A): You decide alone.

Consultative (C): You consult others on the decision but then decide alone.

Group-based (G): A collective decision is made.

Based on what you know so far, would you say you're mainly A, C, or G when it comes to making decisions?

Still not sure?

What may help is to now look at some decision-making preferences, using the **Vroom–Yetton model**.

This defines five different decision-making styles:

A1: You take known information and then decide alone.

A2: You get information from others, and then decide alone.

C1: You share the problem with others individually, listen to ideas and then decide alone.

C2: You share the problems with others as a group, listen to ideas, and then decide.

G2: You share problems with others as a group and then seek and accept consensus agreement.

So, which style are you?

You might be a blend of A1 and C2 or depending on the decision, perhaps you're more G2.

The type of decision you need to make will depend on the style you choose.

If you need to decide how the day's work is to be allocated, you probably don't want to invoke G2; after all, your team will have their own thoughts on who should do what. You need to consider the bigger picture, get information from other sources and then make the decision yourself (A2).

As with all leadership and management skills, there isn't necessarily a best way to make a decision (although there may be a wrong way!)

Be aware of your own preferences and make sure that you use a style that is appropriate to the decision you are making.

Decision-making made easier

OK, so you have your first decision to make, and you know:

- It's Operational
- You can make it (so it's de-centralised)
- You have an Enquiry Mindset

Analysing these three factors, you can pinpoint that it's going to require a C2 decision style. This is because you need to share the problems with others as a group, listen to ideas and then decide. You can select the correct style by applying this process to any decision you need to make.

Here are some additional tips from the Chartered Management Institute (CMI) that I have used over the years. You will also find they reflect some of the decision-making styles we've just covered:

1. Be clear about the scope of the decision you are faced with
2. Consider the potential impact of the decision and how this will be evaluated
3. Decide who needs to be involved in the decision-making process

4. Define the issue to be decided and collect relevant information
5. Take account of uncertainty
6. Gather appropriate contributions
7. Use decision-making tools that fit the situation
8. Watch out for biases and common psychological traps
9. Communicate the decision and act on it
10. Monitor and learn from the outcomes

Psychological bias in decision-making

I want to touch briefly on biases and common psychological traps when it comes to decision-making.

It's a big topic and is relevant to making decisions as a manager but I don't want to overwhelm you with too much information and so, this quote from mindtools.com explains it succinctly:

Psychological bias is the tendency to make decisions or take action in an unknowingly irrational way. To overcome it, look for ways to introduce objectivity into your decision-making, and allow more time for it.

For example, you might subconsciously make selective use of data, or you might feel pressured to decide by powerful colleagues.

Psychological bias is the opposite of common sense and clear, measured judgment. It can lead to missed opportunities and poor decision-making.

Use tools that help you assess background information systematically, surround yourself with people who will challenge your opinions, and listen carefully and empathetically to their views – even when they tell you something you don't want to hear.

You can use tools such as the Vroom-Yetton model, complete a self-assessment or ask a trusted colleague or mentor to assess your own decision-making using the Advocacy and Enquiry mindset examples.

The possible pitfalls in decision-making

You'll know by now that there are advantages, disadvantages, and pros and cons to this whole decision-making process.

So, let's explore some possible pitfalls when it comes to decision-making.

1. **Excluding those who should be involved in decision-making**
    - You could be missing out on knowledge or key information

- And by excluding key people, you can wave goodbye to all that time you've spent building good relationships with them

2. Information overload
- Trying to consider every piece of available information before making a decision until you don't know if you're coming or going
- This can quickly turn to procrastination – trust your gut

3. Analysis paralysis
- This can happen if you have a fear of choosing or making the wrong decision
- If you are prone to overthinking and over-analysing the data, you won't be able to make the decision and may even miss opportunities

4. Common biases
- Failing to recognise common biases in your thinking that might skew decision-making.
- Focusing on the wrong things or failing to seek out relevant information is a sign of biases in decision-making
- Especially if you focus on the thing that confirms only your opinion, so don't get stuck in this cycle, but consider other people's opinions and findings

5. Not monitoring the outcome of the decision
- All decisions have consequences or impact the company in some way, some in a large way and some small

- It's important that you monitor the outcome of your decision and learn from the results. That is not to say it will be a negative outcome – you need to celebrate the positive outcomes too.
- Monitoring is a really important aspect of good management, and this includes monitoring in the decision-making process!

"Fortitude" = Courage, Bravery and Strength

Dealing with other people's decision-making

I have been on the receiving end of many decisions made by my bosses over the years about organisational structure change. As a manager, my role was to implement those decisions. However hard that was, it was important to focus on the decisions that needed to be taken that were for the benefit of the organisation.

I remember one decision in 2013 that brought me to tears in front of my peers, colleagues, and team members, when a senior member of staff informed us all that a restructure and redundancy was coming. I remember the feeling like it was yesterday. The organisation knew change was coming, driven by government funding reductions and a need for the organisation to consolidate and streamline. However, it did not prevent my emotions from showing.

While expressing emotion in front of my team may not be considered an appropriate level of Emotional Intelligence (this is covered in Chapter 8) it showed them I was human and that I was affected by the announcement, so it was more of a positive than a negative.

Once the initial shock and upset settled, I set up team meetings to discuss the way forward.

We all understood the need for change, the need for reductions in budget, resources, and the need for the whole organisation to streamline services and products.

My role as a manager

My role was to manage the change and make informed decisions so that the senior team had considered all the options to take forward. How did I do that? By building on the trust and open approach I had built up over five years, I explored opportunities with key stakeholders, team members, and service users. I identified alternative team structures which would give the department the best chance of sustainability in a changing financial landscape.

While I, as part of the process, like other team members, was going to exit the organisation, I believed that my role was to support the team and see the changes through. I led the process, informed the senior team of operational decisions, made recommendations, and identified key areas of future development. I am proud to say that the decisions I took, however hard I found them, were the right ones for the organisation. The team I previously managed, is still strong, fully operational, and they are recognised as professionals in their sector.

I hope that you don't find yourself in this situation as a manager, but if you do, here are my TATTs to help you through. I've put these together using the real-life example that I went through in 2013.

You can adjust them to fit your own situation. If at any point you need support, please reach out to me:

Tracy-Anne@tabarkerassociates.co.uk

TATTs for dealing with other people's decisions

1. **Focus on the decisions** that needed to be taken and understand they are for the benefit of the company.

2. **Know and understand that it is not personal,** to you or anybody. This is what needs to happen for the company.

3. **It's ok to show a level of emotion.** We're only human after all and you've built great relationships with your team, so some decisions will affect you emotionally.

4. **Add others' perspectives.** Don't stew alone about the choices in front of you. Talk to your line manager or someone you trust about the decision and your assessment. Get things clear in your own head before you speak to your team.

5. **Set up meetings with your teams** as soon as possible. Keeping them in the dark or waiting only adds to upset, causes additional worry or anxiety, and leads to uncertainty.

6. **Anticipate your team's reaction.** Think about how they will react or what they will ask so you can prepare yourself mentally and have answers for the questions.

7. **Explain to your team clearly the need for change,** the need for reductions, resources, or whatever it is that affects them. Avoid words like 'might' 'maybe' 'sort of' as this leads to ambiguity.

8. **Recognise resistance** and allow your team the time to air it. Usually when people are frustrated or angry and say their piece, the negative feelings soon dissipate, and they will then be able to discuss the situation more rationally.

9. **Be open to their questions** and answer as honestly as you can. If you don't know the answer to a question, now is not the time to wing it. Be honest, tell them you will come back to them, and set a timescale as to when this will be.

10. **Focus on the future.** In these situations, it can be quite easy to turn to wallowing in pity or belabouring the issue. So, once your team have aired their feelings and asked questions, help your team to see the new future and what it will look like for them.

And finally, managing decisions like this is challenging, which is why it's so important to have established relationships with your team, open communication, respect for each other, and to know and understand each individual team member.

Decision-making tools and techniques

I hope you've found my tips and advice useful. There are many additional tools and techniques out there to help you with your decision-making. You might want to take a look at these recommended by the CMI:

1. Edward de Bono – Six Thinking Hats
2. Tannenbaum and Schmidt leadership continuum
3. Stakeholder analysis
4. Force field analysis

Or if your role requires you to make data-informed decisions, Qlik have written an article on the Essential Steps to making better data informed decisions, along with the useful diagram below. You'll find a link to the article in the bibliography on page 186

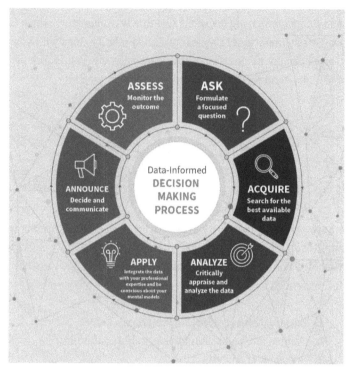

glik.com/blog/essential-steps-to-making-better-data-informed-decisions

It's always good to have a few things in your manager's toolkit, so find what's right for you, your company, your role, and your team.

You will need to adapt over time but isn't that what being a manager is all about?!

Tracy-Anne's Tool Kit Takeaways

This is a quick reference guide to refer to if you're struggling with the decision-making process or if you want to support your team with theirs.

Photocopy this or make your own version to stick on your desk, and it'll become your best friend.

Type	Operational, Tactical, Strategic
Define	Centralised, De-centralised
Decide	Advocacy, Enquiry, or a blend of both
Choose	Mindset A, C, G or a mix of these
Act	Define the issue, collect relevant information, take account of uncertainty, watch out for biases, communicate the decision, and act.
Monitor outcomes	Learn from, celebrate and reward

Group Decision-making Game

Making decisions as a group can be tricky, with all those differing opinions, personalities, and mindsets. This is where decision-making tools really help, especially Edward de Bono's Six Thinking Hats.

The Six Thinking Hats teaches you how to separate thinking into six clear functions and roles. Each thinking role is identified with a coloured symbolic 'thinking hat'. By mentally wearing and switching 'hats', you can easily focus or redirect thoughts, the conversation, or the meeting.

This helps people to be more productive, focused, and mindfully involved*

From* www.debonogroup.com/services/core-programs/six-thinking-hats

You can learn more about the Hats and the Thinking Functions here; as this book is not in colour, you of course just need to visualise the hat colours!

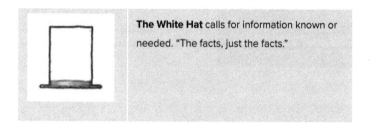

The White Hat calls for information known or needed. "The facts, just the facts."

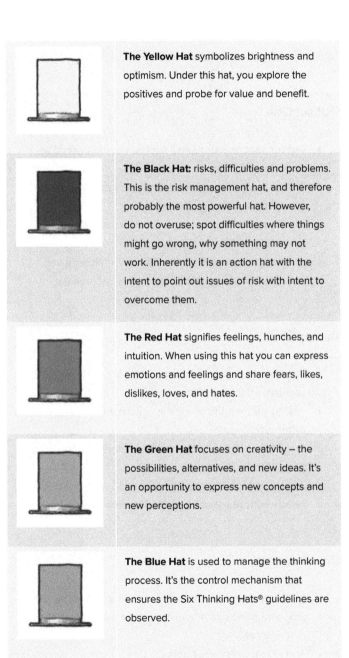

The Yellow Hat symbolizes brightness and optimism. Under this hat, you explore the positives and probe for value and benefit.

The Black Hat: risks, difficulties and problems. This is the risk management hat, and therefore probably the most powerful hat. However, do not overuse; spot difficulties where things might go wrong, why something may not work. Inherently it is an action hat with the intent to point out issues of risk with intent to overcome them.

The Red Hat signifies feelings, hunches, and intuition. When using this hat you can express emotions and feelings and share fears, likes, dislikes, loves, and hates.

The Green Hat focuses on creativity – the possibilities, alternatives, and new ideas. It's an opportunity to express new concepts and new perceptions.

The Blue Hat is used to manage the thinking process. It's the control mechanism that ensures the Six Thinking Hats® guidelines are observed.

There are various ways to use the Six Thinking Hats:

Option One

- Put forward to your team a problem or situation that requires a decision
- Assign yourself the blue hat and every member of the group the SAME coloured hat
- Ensure the rules are observed and record the results, then present them back to the group
- Ask the group what they thought and whether it was beneficial that they all had the same-coloured hat

Option Two

- Put forward to your team a problem or situation that requires a decision
- Assign yourself the blue hat and each individual member a different coloured hat
- Ensure the rules are observed and record the results, then present them back to the group
- Ask the group what they thought and whether it was beneficial that they all had the different coloured hats

Option Three

- Assign yourself the blue hat and depending on the group size, you could assign two people the red hat, two the green, etc etc.
- And repeat the process above.

Option Four

- Assign a member of the team the blue hat
- Allocate the hat colours
- Observe and record the results

This is a great option for any budding managers and for the development of your individual team members.

Outcomes

Similar to the Vroom-Yetton model, the team and you must realise you all have different mindsets and ways of seeing and approaching problems.

Recognising each individual's strengths will result in a harmonious team and will help them to be more productive, focused, and mindfully involved. Just as Edward de Bono set out.

Six Thinking Hats for Managers

As a manager, sometimes you need to wear all the hats when making a decision, so this is another handy tool for your toolkit to print out and keep!

Remember, *"Good decisions come from experience and experience comes from making bad decisions"*.

We can't always be in control of the decisions. Sometimes as a manager our role is how we execute the action with honesty, compassion, and building on the trust we have built with our team.

CHAPTER 7

Stepping Up

Being the captain or boss lady

OR AS SOME may call it, how to manage friends, the pitfalls and challenges, and not overstepping the mark!

First, I would like to address a question that I am asked frequently – "Is there a difference between how male and female bosses react?"

Yes of course, biologically and emotionally there can be, as there are differences between the genders. However, in my experience, this is not a gender issue. Every manager can be different, just as every team member can be different.

We know that in recent years from gender pay gap reports, males were previously paid more than females, and while this is slowly improving, a survey in 2021 from the Yale School of Management has revealed that, despite women having higher performance ratings than men, they were incorrectly judged as having less leadership potential.

Often, leadership and management traits are talked about as assertiveness, delivery of skills, charisma, leadership strength, ambition, and focus. If these traits are measured, they can be subjective and be stereotypically linked to male leadership. Whereas, in my experience, organised communication, passion, nurturing, decisiveness, approachability, and professionalism are very good leadership traits and skills which may appear stereotypically linked to female leadership.

As you will know from this book already, this is not a management book about the differences in gender. It is my experience that while biologically some people may react, respond or act in a particular 'way', don't be surprised, be open to how YOU are, regardless of your gender. We are all different, so please don't put yourself or your team in a gender box.

There can be many obstacles to stepping up to be the captain. And if you've established good friendships with people who were previously your peers, this can be a big moment. But don't worry, I'm going to tell you how to strike the right balance of Parent-Adult-Child transactions (I'll explain more about this shortly) when it comes to communicating and interacting with your team, along with TATTs to ease that transition.

So, if you have just been promoted to a management role, hooray! Congratulations! You are now part of the management team and officially in charge of a team who were previously your peers. OK, how are you going to handle this?

"It's not whether you get knocked down, it's whether you get back up"

Understanding the ego state

I mentioned above, Parent-Adult-Child, and this links to the **'Ego' state.** Let me explain in more detail.

This will give you an understanding of the role you now play in relation to your team.

Parent	A parent represents authority and a caring role. It assumes knowledge about how things are done. Usually, this is displayed in two ways: • Critical, disciplinarian and judgemental • Nurturing, protective and soothing
Adult	Adult represents rational, objective and positive communication. Often mediating between the parent and child parts of our personality
Child	The child aspect is spontaneous, compulsive, irrational, creative, playful and intuitive, and is generally displayed in two ways: • Dutiful, submissive and obedient • Free or irrational, creative and attention-seeking

(Summarised from *Transactional Analysis* by E.Berne)

You were previously on the same level as your peer, so there was very little conflict. Now, as the manager, it is likely that you will be subconsciously viewed as the parent and so the team member may potentially display a child ego state.

It will take time for the team to settle, for you to develop your management style and for you to begin to understand the individuals within your team. As the manager, supervisor or team leader, it is important you begin at the beginning, get to know them, build a picture of their motivators, their strengths and areas of development, and understand how they want to develop in their roles. Never assume you already know all of this!

There are three main styles of transaction that can develop between people in a manager – team member relationship, depending on the adoption of Parent (P), Adult (A) or Child (C) ego state:

Complementary transactions

This is the healthiest for all individuals involved and creates the most productive transaction between two people. Each person is interacting while in the same ego state:

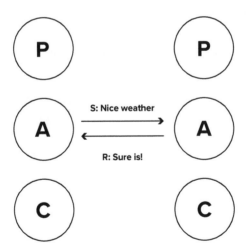

Crossed transactions

These can cause confusion and are the reason why we sometimes find ourselves in conflict or in uncomfortable situations:

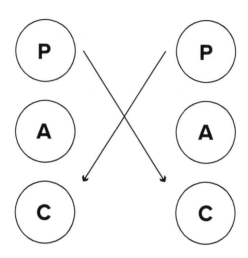

Ulterior transactions

These are the most destructive and difficult to deal with:

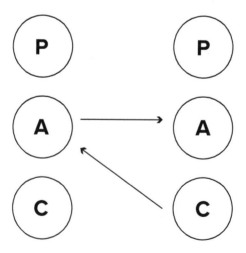

The images demonstrate that when transactions are peer to peer, ie Parent to Parent, Adult to Adult, and Child to Child they are more harmonious and in tune.

Transactional analysis is a collection of concepts that can help you better understand yourself and others. Taking this into account in your new management role can help you to improve your communication skills.

The pain of losing a friend

A man walks into a bar.
The bartender notices how sad he looks and asks, "You OK?"
"I just lost my best friend," says the man.
"How'd it happen?"
"I became his boss."

Does this sound familiar? I know this feeling.

Over 20 years ago, when I gained my first work promotion to a team supervisor, I didn't handle it well. I had the euphoria of the promotion, the delight of a small pay rise, and moved to a new office to join the new team.

I blindly walked in on Monday morning expecting the great relationships I had fostered as a colleague to continue. Hell, no! That was not the case.

Carol had been my friend as a colleague – we would share break times, lunchtimes, and socialise after work – was not happy for me. Suddenly, I was one of 'them', the 'bosses', so I was no longer a trusted confidante and friend.

I was usually the person who made the team brews at 10am, but when I asked Carol, her usual cheery "Yes please, tea with two" response was now a glare and a retort, "Oh, you are still able to get them, not too important are you?"

My heart sank, I felt awkward and alone, and, even worse, the three others in the office did not stick up for me or speak out, and usually, we had been a tight team, so this all came as a shock.

The relationship with Carol never recovered to its previous level – she continued to be hostile and uncooperative. I tried hard with all the team, being supportive, communicating clearly and positively. I worked hard at offering autonomy, identifying team projects, and being approachable. BUT I had made too many assumptions and tried to be their friend too early on as a manager.

Managing a team that is made up of people who were previously your peers can be a tough situation to navigate. A good place to start is with open and honest conversations.

Understanding relationships and realising that we do not all react or behave the same in given situations, or even for the same reasons, will help you identify shifts in behaviour. Also, it will help you spot if there is an underlying motive.

It really is tough to be a friend on a Friday and then the manager on Monday. Your team will know that you need to provide constructive feedback on a performance issue at some stage. Therefore, as you step into that role you need to change your tone to become that of a leadership style.

I recall holding a meeting once with a new team, some of who I knew outside of the office. Both in the meeting but also on a one-to-one basis I told them, "As your manager, I'm still here for you. We're here to work together, I want to see you achieve, and the team and the company succeed. My goal is to provide you with skills and guidance so you will get promoted and help you progress!"

It was important that I acknowledged the change and let them know I had 'their backs' in the 'scrum' of business life. However, my message was that I could no longer tolerate gossiping or moaning. And that we would foster a culture of can do's rather than can't do.

Being professional, focusing on supporting them, helping to support their progress, will also help you to adjust if you witness any of your direct reports acting jealously or being resentful of your promotion. Adopting this outlook made a huge difference to the success of my transition from peer to manager.

TATTs to ease your transition from teammate to manager

1. **First, make the tough call.** Loyalty to work must come before loyalty to your friend. If it can't, you shouldn't be leading that individual.

2. **Set clear boundaries and expectations.** Do not discuss work with friends outside of work.

3. **Be rational, fair and objective.** Treat your friend the same as you would anyone else in your team while at work.

4. **Remember, true friends won't want you to compromise** your work responsibilities; they'll want you to succeed. They won't force you to choose between friendship and work.

5. **Don't confuse being liked** with being trusted and respected.

6. **Break habits you previously had.** If you went to lunch or breaks together with your friend, you do not need to stop doing this, but make it less frequent while staying friendly.

7. **Don't be hard on yourself.** It is highly likely you will have a challenge with the transition at some time.

8. **Tackle the ball, not the player.** Even if it feels personal.

9. **Learn lessons and evaluate what you can do differently.** If and when things go wrong, pick yourself up, dust yourself down and take the steps needed to move forward.

10. **Support your team.** And lastly, remember that being the manager doesn't mean you now have power and control. It means you're responsible for supporting the success of every single individual in your team. You are there to guide, support and foster your team to grow and improve.

Being a manager can be tricky, but there are skills you can develop and tips and hints that can support you in your role. Don't feel alone, reach out for support.

My friend Jack, who I used to work with, recommended that I share this story. I take it as an indicator that I was able to successfully navigate the friend-to-boss journey. When I was at Bluewater and made the transition from peer to boss, one of my team members, Hazel, started calling me 'Boss Lady' very early on. At first, I was a little embarrassed. But I realised it was a nice way for her to acknowledge the situation almost in a half-jokey way, but one that was still underpinned by respect and acceptance. So much so that, fast-forward to now and she still calls me Boss Lady and yet we stopped working together over ten years ago!

You can still be friendly with your team, you can socialise with them, be supportive and caring, if you create the right culture. Those that respect you as a good person, are good at their job and want the best for the team and organisation will respect that you are the boss and that you have responsibilities. They will be happy and supportive of you. Unlike the situation with Carol, I handled this one much better.

Recap on stepping up

A bit of grounding in the theory of Parent – Adult – Child ego states may help you to navigate what can be a tricky period, so it's important to remember:

- You may be viewed as the parent and the team member may display a child ego.
- When transactions are peer to peer, ie Adult to Adult they're more harmonious.

- It will take time for the team to settle, to develop your management style, and to understand the individuals.

Tracy-Anne's Tool Kit Takeaways

Stepping up to a promotion – are you ready?

This is designed to help you identify if you are ready for that new promotion. Score yourself based on your current skill and ability on a scale of 1-4, with 4 being high

- ☐ I deliver on my goals consistently and monitor progress weekly
- ☐ I am crystal clear on my goals and can explain them to others with clarity and consistency
- ☐ I am considerate and patient of others' views and opinions
- ☐ I do not discriminate against others
- ☐ I build good relationships at work that are trustworthy and professional
- ☐ I have a positive professional approach in my relationships with co-workers
- ☐ I am or have been coaching or mentoring co-workers, with successful outcomes
- ☐ I do not play favourites or politicise points at work
- ☐ I take responsibility for my own professional development at work
- ☐ I tackle difficult tasks and do not shy away from challenges
- ☐ I am punctual and on time regularly

- [ ] I use a little humour and have some fun in the workplace
- [ ] I am proactive and positive in team meetings
- [ ] I have good oral and written communication skills
- [ ] When I raise a problem, I offer a solution
- [ ] I am committed to high-quality work, and helping my colleagues and my manager achieve as a department/team
- [ ] I have a mentor to help me develop my skills

Mostly 4 – You are ready to apply for the next promotion. It is essential you read the job description and person specification so that you can clearly demonstrate your experience, commitment, attitude and behaviours. Consider using the S.T.A.R technique. It can be a really useful way to answer an application or use in an interview.

- **S.** **Situation:** Describe the situation and when it took place
- **T.** **Task:** Explain the task and what was the goal
- **A.** **Action:** Provide details about the action you took to attain this
- **R.** **Result:** Conclude with the result of your action

Good luck!

Combination of 3 and 4 – you are almost ready. Increasing your skills to improve the quantity of 4s is essential so that you can be a stronger applicant.

Combination of 1 to 3 – you have some areas to work on, so plan these into your Continuing Professional Development (CPD) during the next 6-12 months. Improving your skills and abilities will support future promotion applications.

Don't forget: If you are looking for a supportive group of managers who will champion and support you, with online resources you can use to develop your skills, check out The Managers' Circle, full details are in the bibliography.

Transition checklist

Helping you move from A–Z when gaining your promotion:

Photocopy or write down this checklist and keep it somewhere you can refer to in the early days of your promotion.

Trust me, it will make your transition much easier and will become the groundwork for everything else in this book:

- [ ] Change your tone to a leadership style and bring back the balance
- [ ] Set clear boundaries and expectations
- [ ] Treat everyone the same
- [ ] Get to know each individual, and don't assume you already know them
- [ ] Be fair and objective
- [ ] Break old habits
- [ ] There is a difference between being liked and being trusted and respected. Make sure you recognise it.

Psychological safety

This is another topic I want to cover in this chapter, as it is a term you may hear from time to time. I have been training a group of managers recently to embed this in the culture of their organisation. But what does it mean?

Before I knew the term, I have always been focused on creating a culture where people can speak their minds, speak up, be transparent, honest, and feel safe within their team. And, importantly, when team members do speak up, there are no repercussions or consequences for speaking truthfully. That is psychological safety.

Unfortunately, that is not always the case in many workplace settings. When team members are not comfortable talking about things that are not working well, an organisation will not be fully equipped to prevent failure. When they are not motivated, and I talk more about this in Chapter 4, or when they are not committed to your organisation, you really cannot get the most out of the team, increase productivity and maximise performance.

Ultimately, as the captain, it is your role to support and develop your team, helping them to maximise performance so your business can be successful and sustainable. I am not suggesting that psychological safety means that you create an environment where everyone is merely nice to each other all the time. Instead, I believe you should foster a culture that encourages honesty, openness and transparency. One that enables people to speak up, knowing that their team has their back and that you as their manager has their backs. You need to facilitate your team being able to speak up by creating a structure for handling failure and by creating space for new ideas to emerge.

If you and your team are motivated to perform and committed to the organisation, establishing a psychologically safe culture will aid productive conflict and progress. So, what's not to like about creating this type of culture?

I remember a situation shared with me by my good friend Angela, she had first-hand experience in a previous organisation, working with the leadership team, making an attempt at creating a psychological safety culture. There were away days where the whole leadership team contributed to ideas and finally a draft charter was established. The problem was, it turned out to be merely a 'box ticking' exercise. The CEO didn't really commit to it, as he had been asked to set it up by the board. There was no buy-in from the leadership team and no one felt motivated or committed to embracing a true change of culture. Angela described to me the lack of trust and concern that remained at leadership level, a malaise which was felt throughout the organisation.

So, the charter did not get adopted and the organisation did not make any culture changes. In fact, Angela sat in many leadership meetings where the CEO would use the term 'psychological safety' in the most inappropriate terms, further minimising the opportunities to embrace the benefits and safe culture.

It became clear a few years later that this tick box exercise had in fact just been that, a tick-box exercise. When there was a significant incident in the organisation and one brave and honest member of the team spoke up and was transparent and truthful, the CEO did not address the issue. In fact, he and the board swept it under the carpet. This was a perfect example of them not dealing with the challenge. If the organisation had been practising a successful culture of psychological safety, other people would have spoken up and spoken out, and it would not have been that one lone voice. The result of the board and the CEO's inaction was so far-reaching that the organisation imploded, it is no longer in operation, and Angela moved on. Just think about that. It was not the trading situation, the state of the company balance sheet or a lack of customers that led to a whole organisation failing – it was a failure by management to put in place an adequate psychological safety policy and culture. *It's that important.*

People need to feel comfortable in speaking up, disagreeing with the way things are so that change can be implemented, and a real difference can be made.

In my team, creating a safety net, encouraging open discussions and a diversity of ideas and team input in a safe environment with no fear of consequences, is vital.

So, you are there to guide, support and foster each individual team member to grow and improve.

I want to share a story my friend Stephen shared with me recently. It is one that I share with the managers I train and coach. He recalls the difference between two former managers. One was open and transparent and a great communicator, while the other, in contrast, was constantly suspicious, untrusting of the team, unreliable, and made promises that could not be kept that led to further mistrust. Stephen wanted to gain future promotion and was looking for role models to guide his development. He had one good role model and the other inspired him on how not to be a manager. The contrast he compared was the impact the two different managers had as soon as they walked into a room.

When the good role model walked into the room, their face was open, inquisitive and approachable, body language was relaxed and friendly yet professional. Their attire was confident and relevant to the work setting. In contrast, the other had a grumpy and stressed-out appearance, and was messy and unkempt. They constantly folded their arms, and their tone of voice was sharp and often loud.

Organisations are hierarchies of job titles, each performing a job with different responsibilities, managing critical functions of the organisation. The higher the rank, often the further away the person is from the day-to-day operations. A manager's role is to shape the culture and development of their team, help them perform and maximise output.

Gaining your team members' trust and building rapport is vital, and in Chapter 5 we explored relationships in more detail. Not forgetting that managers have the power to hire and fire team members, this fact alone may put people on edge and they may not trust you. If you have not built a good rapport, if you have not developed an open and honest management style, if your demeanour and approach is not correct when you walk into a room, this may result in worry, concern, stress and upset, leading to retention, motivation and performance issues. So, remember your outward appearance, body language, and tone of voice are just as important as your words and actions.

CHAPTER 8

Being Successful

*The secrets of creating a
World Cup winning team*

I HAVE SHARED with you some key areas for you to develop in your management role. In this chapter, we explore how *you* can develop the team. You can't expect to create the equivalent of a rugby World Cup winning team if you don't support, guide and manage their performance. But how do you manage performance?

It's more than just telling someone they've done a great job or giving constructive feedback. What you need is a performance management system. Throughout this chapter, I go into detail about what performance management really is, how you can use it effectively in your team, how to avoid pitfalls, and TATTs to performance-manage like a pro.

I'll also cover why Emotional Intelligence is an important life and business skill, and how to develop your own EI. I have also included a section on the importance of self-reflection. Being able to reflect and review to help progress, performance, and also support our personal wellbeing has been overlooked in recent times. I know that in my early management career I struggled with reflection.

Managing the performance of the team should be a cross-organisation approach, integrated to help the business meet its key aims and objectives.

What is performance management?

It's the monitoring and support of individuals so they can improve individual performance, the team's performance, and the total company performance.

Responsibility for monitoring and then supporting team performance is the role of the manager.

Most businesses will have a system to set up and agree targets and objectives, therefore enabling managers to measure and review performance.

This would usually start with the HR processes. It may be an annual appraisal; in more recent times many businesses have switched to twice-yearly reviews or appraisals.

It's important, that a manager helps an individual team member to understand the performance management process. So that they can contribute positively to aid any performance improvements and achievement of aims and objectives towards the wider organisational goals.

What is a Performance Management System?

A performance management system includes agreed targets and objectives to enable managers to measure, monitor and review performance. This provides clarity on the contribution that the individual is making towards the achievement of the business goals. If there are gaps, then managers and the team member can work to narrow them through achievement and performance.

To be an effective performance review, whether yearly, twice yearly, quarterly or monthly, it should be conducted in line with the organisation's overall strategic plan. This ensures that the team or individual is working towards the common business goals.

How do I support, guide and manage my team through a performance review?

Like most things in life, a bit of pre-planning goes a long way. I recommend the following checklist:

- [ ] Elements that you pre-plan – E.g., annual, twice-yearly, etc.
- [ ] Regular reviews, either informal or formal.
- [ ] Feedback for individuals, teams, and the organisation via 360-degree feedback.
- [ ] A shared process between manager and employee.
- [ ] Agreement of clear, challenging yet achievable targets.
- [ ] Support and developmental opportunities.
- [ ] Monitoring, reviewing, and renewing of goals.
- [ ] Celebration of success, and accountability for improvements.

Things to avoid:

- Providing unachievable targets. You should build target steps that support a larger objective.
- Being inflexible, rigid, or dictating goal setting. It's important to gain buy-in.
- Expecting a quick fix.

- Surprising employees about poor performance. Issues need to be addressed early.
- Neglecting soft skill development. E.g., building relationships and giving feedback.

Define and identify

You need to define what you want from your business, including your goals, as once you have clarity on these you can then build your staff strategy around them.

TATTs to help you develop a World Cup winning team

1. **Align individual targets** with the organisation or department strategy.

2. **Set standards and measures** to indicate the progress of the target – ensure they are SMART*.

3. **Ensure clarity and transparency** by having a clear evaluation method for performance.

4. **Build performance appraisals** into your business cycle.

5. **Do not be ambiguous:** Communicate clearly and concisely about performance management.

6. **Monitor and review performance** at regular intervals.

7. **Address poor performance:** Do not surprise employees or delay but tackle it early.

8. **Support team members** to develop the skills and knowledge required to achieve their targets.

9. **Give feedback** and ensure it is clear and suitable.

10. **Celebrate success** and learn from areas of development.

Communication is key throughout the cycle. Luckily this book is full of useful TATTs and examples of how to communicate effectively in any situation.

*SMART – Specific, Measurable, Achievable, Realistic, Timebound.

Staff training

One final point to consider within your Performance Management Framework: Is your staff training in a good place?

Regulatory and legislative training is usually a key focus for the business. Your team could also benefit from other programmes that support people's development and the building of knowledge. Examples are managing staff, staff motivation, time management, appraisals and reviews, absence management, and conflict and resolution management.

Checklist for Performance Management in your business

Now it's over to you, so go through this checklist and any that you don't tick, that's where you need to place your focus. This may involve having to approach your manager and instigate change.

- ☐ Are you familiar with your business's Performance Management System?
- ☐ Are individual targets aligned with the business's/ department strategy and goals?
- ☐ Are the targets SMART?
- ☐ Does your business have development opportunities?
- ☐ Does your team have regular performance reviews?
- ☐ Is feedback encouraged between all teams and departments?
- ☐ Do you give clear, effective feedback regularly?

Also be mindful that the ones you have ticked, may also need looking into – don't be afraid to challenge the system. If you do, remember to put forward ideas of what any alternatives could look like.

Tracy-Anne's Tool Kit Takeaways

Performance Management

Inspired by Sheridan Webb, the practical training designer

There are four types of typical problems you'll encounter when looking at the underperformance of a team member or team:

- A lack of knowledge
- A lack of skill
- A lack of will
- A lack of resources or poor processes

And it can be easy to assume you know what the problem is. Don't assume.

Use open questioning techniques to identify if there is a requirement to:

- Tell or educate
- Train
- Motivate, influence, and persuade
- Solve a problem

This visual helps to explain the process further:

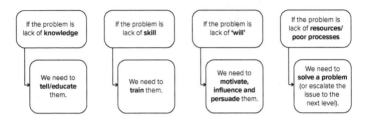

Let me explain a little further about performance of a team in business compared to that of a rugby team. I use this in training with managers I work with.

Diversity: It would be a really boring world if we were all the same, a carbon copy of each other, all doing the same things. It is evidenced by the diverse nature of a rugby team where there is a place for all sizes, shapes, and speeds. If the whole team was built around the strength and bulk of the forwards, it would not be an all-round strong performing team. While it would win the scrums through size and strength, it would be too slow in open play and struggle to score tries.

The division of labour, roles and specialisms between beefy forwards and speedy backs, is essential to the game. Just as with a team in business, led by the manager, a team is formed of different roles with different levels of experience and responsibility. If everyone was a supervisor and there were no team members to undertake the daily tasks, the team would not be effective.

Once you have your team formed, to aid them in their individual roles managing their performance is vital.

Emotional Intelligence for managers (EI): What it REALLY means ...

A few years ago, Emotional Intelligence was quite a buzz phrase where I worked, but many people clearly didn't understand its full meaning (including me). So, what is EI?

According to Daniel Goleman, there are five principal areas of EI and, like many skills, it can be developed.

The Five Goleman principles

1. Self-awareness
2. Self-regulation
3. Motivation
4. Empathy
5. Social skills

But what does it all mean?!

Don't worry, I'm going to tell you.

Here's my own interpretation of the principles ...

Self-awareness

A good manager needs to understand the impact of using self-awareness techniques to produce results, and this means:

- Having an awareness of the impact you have on other people and developing the areas you need to improve.
- Understanding your own areas of strength, and requirements for development.
- Understanding how your emotions impact your team.

Self-regulation

Controlling your own emotions and being accountable for your actions. This requires the following:

- It's important that you reflect on your ability and behaviours. Good leaders demand much of themselves as well as their teams and don't foster a blame culture.
- Thinking before you act, not just responding to a knee-jerk reaction.
- Knowing your own values and beliefs; think about what matters to you and how you want to be perceived.
- Using mindfulness techniques or meditation to help you regulate any unwanted emotional responses in difficult situations.

Motivation

EI people are self-motivated and good at motivating others. It's therefore important that you understand your team and tailor motivational actions for each individual to get the best out of your team.

If you need a recap on this issue, check back on Chapter 4.

I have worked with someone who I consider to be the best type of leader and he was relentlessly positive, focused, and had a clear vision of the necessary direction of travel for the business. He used this to drive action, look to the future, and did not dwell or over-analyse the past.

Empathy

I believe this is one of the most important principles of EI – your ability to put yourself in someone else's shoes.

- This can give you insights into why some of your team might be underperforming and how they can be nurtured and coached to improve.
- Being genuinely interested in other people, asking questions about goals and how they might wish to develop, are all great signs of empathy.

Social skills

As an EI manager, the ability to communicate is key, and this means:

- Being able to communicate with a range of different audiences and situations.

- Communicating good and bad news and managing challenging situations.
- Being a captain at conflict resolution management techniques.

"Victory is the goal, Determination gets you there"

Self-reflection

As mentioned before, in my early management career I struggled with personal reflection. It wasn't a skill that came naturally. The Berkeley Well-Being Institute defines it as *"wanting to know why you do the things you do"*. www.berkeleywellbeing.com/what-is-self-reflection

My interpretation of this is: Self-reflection is the ability to review what works well, what works less well, and how you can develop and progress.

Reflecting on a topic, subject or activity can help you to gain perspective by allowing you to step back. This can result in you making better and more informed decisions. Using self-reflection, I have found, by understanding myself better, I can better understand my team.

Have you ever heard the expression, *The definition of insanity is doing the same thing over and over again and expecting a different result.*

These words are usually credited to the acclaimed genius Albert Einstein. If we want to improve and progress in our management roles, self-reflection is vital.

Tracy-Anne's Top Tips on self-reflection

So, it is **TATTs** time, and here are my suggestions for helping you to improve your self-reflection skills and in turn build your Emotional Intelligence.

These will help you reflect on your strengths and areas for development, which in turn will help you with all five of the principles of Emotional Intelligence. Developing these over time will support your ability, skill and progress.

1. **Take time.** Build reflective time into your day. Work out when will suit you and then make it a regular habit. It should be something you do frequently, so don't leave it or just try to cram it in.

2. **Write it down.** Have a notebook, either physical or electronic, when you are taking regular time to reflect. Write your thoughts down – what went well, what could be developed, what could you do better. It's important to note your successes too, to revisit and reflect on in the future.

3. **Give it attention.** Your reflection time is important, so turn off your phone, close your emails and minimise any

distractions. Focus on the practice of reflection, give it your undivided attention.

4. **Pace.** If you are someone that finds slowing down and taking time out for yourself and your personal development difficult, consider mindfulness or meditation. Your own development is just as important as the development of your team. Make space to slow down and give yourself the time and space to reflect so that you can grow and improve.

5. **No judgment.** Approach your reflection without self-criticism or judgment. Don't beat yourself up about the things that did not go well.

6. **Celebrate success.** Identify what has gone well and reflect on what could be different next time.

7. **Experiment with different tools.** The CIPD has a range of suggested tools to help with a reflective practice including freewriting, free drawing, and have a great question bank to help you with your reflective practice. www.cipd.co.uk/Images/reflective-practice-guide_ tcm18-12524.pdf

8. **Identify a champion, mentor, coach or buddy.** Just as buddy systems for your team can provide a great support framework within your organisation, having a mentor is good practice for managers to help them develop, grow and gain critical feedback to support their development. A mentor can be internal or external to your organisation. Importantly, they need to be able to

support you with reflective practice and constructive feedback.

9. **Communicate your areas for development** clearly with your line manager, your team and your supporters. Ask them for support to help you.

10. **Take action.** Sitting staring at your reflective notes will not help you progress or move forward. Identifying what you need to do differently, what behaviours you need to retain and those you need to change are important, as is your next step in taking action. Do not leave your thoughts in your reflective journal but decide which first steps you need to take to move forward.

There is no magic wand, no one size fits all answer to developing yourself and helping your team to develop too. However, reflective practice is a great starting point if you want to develop your skills, your practice and become an Emotionally Intelligent Manager.

And remember, if you don't want to foster a culture of long hours don't work long hours. If you want collaboration, share your unfinished work and seek feedback.

Why not teach your team these principles now, rather than waiting until they are ready for promotion? The sooner you introduce your team to EI, the better prepared they will be for future career opportunities, and who wouldn't want an emotionally intelligent team that hits the ball out of the park continuously and displays epic teamwork?!

Tracy-Anne's Tool Kit Takeaways

Using Emotional Intelligence in the most practical sense may not be easy if emotions are heightened. Using an acronym for following as a quick checker can help us stabilise our feelings if the situation is challenging. Like all tools and processes, the more we use them, the more familiar and second nature they become.

FRIDA is a great one to use, developed by my colleague Sheridan Webb, give it a go!

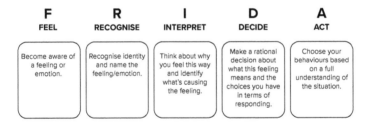

F FEEL	**R** RECOGNISE	**I** INTERPRET	**D** DECIDE	**A** ACT
Become aware of a feeling or emotion.	Recognise identity and name the feeling/emotion.	Think about why you feel this way and identify what's causing the feeling.	Make a rational decision about what this feeling means and the choices you have in terms of responding.	Choose your behaviours based on a full understanding of the situation.

And, finally, here is a checklist that I use with the managers I train and coach, give it a go.

It would be great to hear how you find it, so feel free to get in touch:

Tracy-Anne@tabarkerassociates.co.uk

Developing your EI checklist

- [ ] Build reflective time in your day and give it the attention it deserves
- [ ] Record your thoughts and feelings
- [ ] Do not judge yourself – be subjective
- [ ] Consider mindfulness or meditation
- [ ] Access free CIPD tools
- [ ] Get a mentor, coach or buddy
- [ ] Take action

CHAPTER 9

The Gift of Organisation

Organisation = productivity

I HAVE SHARED in the previous chapters important topics to help you develop your management skills and knowledge. In this chapter, I want to share with you a long-held belief in relation to organisation. How do you feel about being organised? Does it fill you with dread or is it a natural state for you?

My belief about organisation goes back to when I was at secondary school. Do you remember me telling you about becoming Head Monitor for Mrs Cogley? She was the most organised teacher I have ever known. She had a place for everything, and her office and resource cupboard were meticulously tidy. I remember going home and asking my mother to purchase an oversized school bag. I then filled it with organised books, pens, folders and stationery and I started my organisation journey. And I am still on that journey today, giving everything a 'place' to be stored: notebooks for a specific use, files, and in-trays for every task and topic. The same applies to my electronic files, with a place for everything, all stored neatly.

Why am I sharing this with you?

Well, being organised is vital if you want to be a highly effective manager.

Achieving future success in your management role will come as a result of your planning and your daily action. Good organisation can really support you in gaining control of your time, enabling you to plan and complete the tasks and activities needed so that you can achieve your goals and objectives.

In a previous management role (you can read about it more in Chapter 10), I travelled extensively across the UK and occasionally internationally. Being organised was vital. It was before the use of platforms like Zoom, Teams, Webex or GoogleMeet. While travelling I still had loads of tasks to complete, clients to speak with, team members to support, business to conduct, and deals to close.

At times, it was a real high-pressure environment. The business owner's wife was my line manager, and she could be a real Jekyll and Hyde. I never knew which mood we were going to face each day. I tried to shield my team from her outbursts and soon realised that her behaviours were not how I wanted to manage others. Don't get me wrong, she had some good traits, but her dark moods affected us all. Why am I sharing this story with you in this chapter about organisation?

As a manager, handling my busy operational role, dealing with office politics, ensuring client satisfaction, cultivating new business, and relationship development, were all crucial to being a highly effective employee. However, I was also a manager of people; and I needed to be highly organised to keep all these different plates spinning, AND make time to support and develop my team, despite how busy or stressed I might have been. After all, a manager's main role is to support and develop their team.

Being organised can help us with another challenge that we sometimes face, overwhelm. If our to-do lists are off the scale or in a mess, if we are unable to plan and use our management skills, we can find ourselves in a cycle of negativity which increases the overwhelm.

Give yourself the gift of organisation

I have used these **TATTs** over the last 20 years – they are tried and tested and help me at moments of overwhelm and stress. They have helped me stay grounded and I hope they will help you with your management organisation.

1. **Set your priorities.** Understanding what your priorities are in your team, your business and how that links to the work your team undertakes is so important to help you with number 2.

2. **Focus on what is important.** Remind yourself of your own, your team, and your business's long-term goals. Set daily priorities to meet those goals.

3. **Make meaningful lists.** Either in a planner or journal, or electronically, note down the daily, weekly, monthly and quarterly important tasks. Review your daily priorities and focus at the beginning of each day.

4. **Manage your time well.** Don't allow time to manage you. Schedule time in your diary to accomplish tasks that need your focus. Make time to do the most challenging tasks when your energy is high. Ensure that you have given time and space to support your team.

5. **Use calendars and planning tools** to plan your time. Check your business calendar daily, as it helps you review what is ahead for the day, and helps you manage

conflicts. Use your diary to plan ahead and schedule time for larger projects.

6. **Define deadlines** for your own work and the work of your team. Being able to plan time in for each piece of work or task will create room for better, more productive organisation.

7. **Set activity or project milestones.** Micromanaging is not a great management trait. Most staff, once trained and confident in a task or role, don't want to be micromanaged. Set milestones and check-in points so that you can support team members at agreed points. Micromanaging is not only stressful and challenging; it creates more work for you!

8. **Learn to delegate well.** Delegation is an important skill for a manager and assigning tasks to team members is vital to develop their skills but also supports you to increase your capacity to deal with other tasks. Be mindful of not delegating rubbish or boring tasks all the time – give the team opportunities to work on interesting or larger projects.

9. **Manage your emails and telephone calls.** Where needed, use voicemail to screen calls for urgency, responding to those that need it in priority order. Don't be a slave to emails – instead, set time aside in your diary to respond in line with your priorities.

10. Declutter, get tidying up. A clear workspace helps you stay on top of what are the most critical and priority actions of the day. Archive files and resources that are no longer needed. Use a tray system or files to organise resources and information that are used frequently. At the end of the day, clear down your workspace, and spend 10-15 minutes planning the activities and priorities for the following day.

"Pride in excellence"

If you are striving to be good at your job, want to be the best team manager you can be, AND have a fulfilling and rewarding job, get organised!

I don't promise you a magic wand – however, it WILL make your management role easier, more streamlined and less overwhelming.

Organisation = productivity

It is a universally accepted fact that productivity in business can help meet company-wide targets and goals. One way managers can support this is to help team members with organisation so that they can focus on key individual tasks. This will allow them time and space to collaborate with colleagues on joint projects and help them meet deadlines.

With an ever-increasing focus on our team's wellbeing, encouraging them to be organised in the workplace is an important aspect to achieving a better work-life balance. They will be more likely to complete tasks during working hours instead of needing to take a project home, work overtime or make work calls and answer emails outside of work. I know that maintaining a work-life balance helps you to get ready to start each new week with a clear mind.

Try this Tracy-Anne Toolkit Takeaway:

Be organised using the 'D' strategy

Here is a strategy that I have found really useful to focus my mind and to help with organisation. I have based it on the Eisenhower matrix, which was named after Dwight Eisenhower, the 34th President of the United States. However, I have adapted it to suit my style, and the managers I train and coach find it a really useful technique.

To start, review your meaningful list, number 3 in the TATTs above.

This technique is based on my principle that if we focus on what WE have to do NOW, and diarise the tasks only WE can do, we can identify if there are tasks we can delegate or even ditch.

So, using this template, put each task on the list into one of these four quadrants:

Do it	Ditch it
Diarise it	**Delegate it**

Delegation

This subject could be included within a number of chapters. However, I have included it here because delegating tasks is a core skill as well as being part of a wider strategic plan. From your perspective it will help you with organisation, as it will help you to improve your time management, reduce your stress levels and help you build trust within your team. However, the wider benefits for the team are increased self-esteem, confidence and a sense of achievement. Ultimately, this leads to increasing productivity and efficiency for the business.

Below is a checklist to help your delegation journey:

Prepare before you delegate: preparation is key

- ☐ Assign tasks to the right people
- ☐ Be specific with the task you are delegating
- ☐ Check understanding and gain commitment
- ☐ Provide training
- ☐ Follow up at checkpoints
- ☐ Don't micromanage employees
- ☐ Offer effective feedback
- ☐ Say thanks and celebrate

Finally, understand that the process of delegation will never be 100% perfect. However, learn from your experiences when delegating and make the necessary adjustments for improvement.

Recap on organisation

Organisation does not come naturally to everyone. Being organised increases productivity, focus and clarity, and provides greater opportunities to achieve targets and goals. All this leads to increased efficiency and results in a happier team environment.

Try some of these strategies to refine your organisation or start on your organisation journey. Encourage a team culture of organisation and you, the team and the business will reap the rewards.

CHAPTER 10

Remote Working, It Is Not New!

Being on the road again

AS I MENTIONED in Chapter 9, in a previous management role, I travelled extensively across the UK and occasionally internationally. All this was before the use of online platforms like Zoom, Teams, Webex or GoogleMeet.

I spent over 70% of my time travelling to client meetings, attending site visits and meeting suppliers. The remaining 30% was challenging. Not only did I have vast mountains of paperwork and administration to complete, I had a team to manage, motivate, support and train. When I look back at this, I can see that early on I was haphazard in my approach. In the beginning, some team members were not fully supported, as I was not finding the time to speak to them, or when I was in the office, I was not making time to meet with them. But I did settle into a rhythm and find my way forward. That came from quickly realising how badly I was affected by poor line management from *my* line manager. This was not something I wanted to inflict upon my team.

I realised:

"It's all about the team"

As a team member, when a line manager does not make time for you, does not support you or value what you have to say and contribute, it can become very difficult and frustrating. The impact is that you can lose direction, become demotivated, and are less effective in your role.

I was being pressurised to achieve a high level of performance from my team to meet business and income targets. It was clear that I could not achieve what we needed without the team performing at an optimum level. Of course, I knew this from previous management roles, but this role was different, with my team dispersed right across the UK. In addition, I had colleagues I needed to liaise with in other countries.

So, I hear you say, "Why are you telling me this?" and "Why are you including this topic in this book?"

Well, it illustrates that remote working is not new! It was happening before the pandemic of 2019/20.

That global shift has made remote working a bigger factor for many organisations, and as a result for managers. But managers like me and maybe you have been managing remote teams for decades.

As I have mentioned above, when team members work remotely, they can be significantly impacted upon by bad line management.

Let's look at this from a manager's perspective – how do you feel about managing remote workers? Do you find it difficult or frustrating?

There are so many good reasons for having remote teams, and I want all managers to benefit from the knowledge of why and how this can be good for business. I want you to avoid falling into the trap of micro-management. I want you to feel that you never need an 'in-house team' again. And I want to share with you the TATTs so you and your team can be successful.

I want to reference a report that I find interesting. It demonstrates that a growing proportion of the workforce population is seeing remote working as the norm. The Mega Trends report by the CIPD in April 2020 showed that, "The proportion of jobs in which people mainly work from home has risen by 80% in the past two decades (1999 – 2019). Approximately one in twenty (5.3%) jobs are worked mainly from home. This represents 1.8 million people."

Of course, the publication was at the beginning of the pandemic, I suspect that the proportion is much higher now. The department for Business, Energy, and Industrial Strategy (BEIS) asked for the learnings of the pandemic to be included in a taskforce study to expand upon this report and the findings are due soon.

I have colleagues that manage teams successfully in the remote working world and they are brilliant at it. Here are some of the thoughts they have shared with me:

Benefits of remote working

1. When you are not restricted to a fixed location, your talent pool widens meaning you can hire the very best employees.
2. Increases diversity within the organisation. Along with the wider talent pool, it encourages the team to have a more outward-facing international and culturally diverse perspective rather than working with people that are local to their location. It can foster great diversity and relationships.
3. Offering employees a flexible remote working option, either at home or from a local co-working space closer to their home, will help reduce your business and staff carbon footprint. It will also help staff reduce their commuting costs, and potentially your business overheads.

4. Various studies and surveys suggest that when the team has the option to work remotely, they have an improved work-life balance. This can increase productivity and wellbeing which will impact positively on output and ultimately save money in staff absence.

5. As well as a reduction in commuting costs, it saves time. Meaning a direct benefit to the employee.

6. It can increase employee retention. If they move location or may consider leaving due to childcare or caring responsibilities, travelling to a fixed location may no longer work for them.

7. Fewer absenteeism issues. If the team members are not commuting to a location, they are unlikely to be delayed by travel restrictions or bad weather challenges that can affect commuting.

So, there you have seven benefits of a good remote working model. It creates business flexibility, cost efficiencies, increased access to a good talent pool, a motivated and engaged team, leading to increased productivity and profitability. Which business would not want that?

With all those positives, you may ask why more businesses don't move to this model.

Remote working blocks

One of the biggest barriers to remote work is trust. Managers simply do not trust their people to work untethered. They are used to managing by counting bums on seats, rather than by results. That is not managing, that is babysitting.

What is more, seeing the back of someone's head tells a manager nothing about whether that person is working in an effective and productive manner.

I remember an example a manager shared with me – they knew 'John' was working because they could see he had his headset on, his fingers were flying over the keyboard and so all was good. The manager had no idea if John was meeting his targets because he was not monitoring them! However, when he explored further, John was not working, he was online using the organisational equipment to run his own business!

Micromanagement does not work and neither does 'managing by walking around' in this global, mobile world. If you have a remote working team, you will need to learn that it's results that matter.

Research shows that managers who have worked at home themselves are more likely to endorse it for others. One of the reasons I am such an advocate for it! Their worries about lost productivity go away. As they and their team get used to using virtual tools, their worries about not being able to collaborate are proven wrong. They see for themselves just how much happier and engaged they are without the stress of commuting, being away from loved ones, workplace interruptions etc.

If you are managing remote teams or individuals, here are some tried and tested TATTs for successful remote management – and it doesn't include one iota of micromanagement!

Tracy-Anne's Remote Working Top Tips

1. **Start as you mean to go on,** with robust recruitment and onboarding.

   New jobs can be scary and even more so if you are not physically in the same location as colleagues. Getting the process right and setting the tone for the future is vital to help the employee feel motivated, excited to work for you, and to start to build trust. Check in with them at the end of each day, support them with questions they might have during their first few weeks.

2. **Explore online tools,** including instant chat functions and virtual meeting technologies.

   There are numerous tools including Zoom, MS Teams, etc. The team needs to have informal and formal conversations with you and your colleagues. Keep chat functions to informal conversations, and never steer into the dangerous territory of formal or even disciplinary conversations on a chat tool.

3. **Set clear deadlines, goals and targets**. Break them down into manageable chunks and follow up either at the beginning or the end of the day or week. Do not leave long gaps between contact and discussing these. Make sure you talk through what has been achieved and agree on any actions if they have not.

4. **Hold regular 1 to 1s.** This allows you to connect with each member of your team, check how they are progressing

with projects, day-to-day work, and build rapport. Keep 1:1s regular and consistent by committing to them in your calendar. They are very important.

Unlike working with a face-to-face team, there are no opportunities for members of a remote team to drop in impromptu to your office. Therefore, this consistency is important to stay up to date on what the remote team is working on and build trust. Where possible these sessions should be virtual video calls such as Zoom, MS Teams, or any other chosen video resource.

5. **Hold virtual team meetings.** As well as regular 1:1 contact, it's important to build up rapport within your team. Enabling teams to feel included, and to allow all the team members to get to know each other, are critical to success. It may even be that you need to handle a blended situation, where part of the team is working together in an office space, and other team members are working remotely. You need to work hard to to create a sense of belonging and community, so that all team members feel equally engaged and involved, no matter what their working arrangements. Use an agenda issued in advance to give structure to virtual meetings and allow individuals to be aware of the topics before the meeting. You could also encourage team members to advise of specific issues before the meeting and ask for their input on topics to discuss.

6. **Be mindful of hours and time zones.** If you have a remote team that works different hours, or across time zones, be mindful and respectful of the team working hours.

Do not schedule meetings outside of working hours. Find a time when the team hours overlap with you and make the necessary arrangements. If you bring the whole team together and there are still challenges for team members to attend, take the time to arrange meetings at alternative times so that in any given period of time team members can join in with the meetings. E.g., do not consistently exclude team members.

If you send messages and instructions or set tasks outside of the team core working hours, you must be clear that you do not expect a response until their working hours start. You will create unnecessary stress if they think you expect them to respond in their own time.

Being clear about expected working times and response times can help with this issue.

7. **Do not manage by email.** Trying to manage projects and tasks over email leads to a sense of Inbox overload, which is unhealthy for businesses and individuals. Choose a tracking tool like Trello, Basecamp, or MS Teams that you and your team can use to gain clarity on the next steps such as expectations, deadlines, and ownership of tasks and activities. Moving your project to a tracking tool can avoid email overload, clutter, confusion and provide a clear visual representation of the project.

8. **Set up a buddy system.** As part of that process of getting the team to work together, get staff speaking either on the telephone or in a virtual meet-up space to help

them support each other, independent of your input as a manager. Encourage relationship building and identify colleagues that are happy to support them and provide feedback.

9. **Encourage a work routine.** Sitting in their PJs all day is not motivational or good for mental health. Set a clear and consistent time for lunch and breaks. Ensure you have provided your teams with the right resources and equipment to work remotely.

10. **Look out for the quiet ones!** As a final note, from experience, this one is worth noting! It's easy to get distracted and have our management attention drawn to the loud and talkative people in our team. After all, if they have any issues or questions, they will more than likely tell you, without much prompting. However, quiet team members may retreat even more when working remotely.

So, as a manager, along with your own strategies for coping with remote workers, it's vital you establish some good communication practice with the team in a way that ensures everyone is included.

Along with the TATTs for managing a remote team you can also incorporate the following six steps:

- **Re real and authentic**: Create and encourage a culture of psychological safety, as this will help team members to be happy and more productive. You can read more about psychological safety in Chapter 7.

- **Use visual icons**: These are designed into many virtual platforms – a good example is the 'hand raise' icon. Make use of these so that it is easy for all team members to contribute and express their views, even those quiet ones who may be less willing to 'jump in' and give their view. A hand raise may be more comfortable.
- **Have everyone on camera:** Encourage the whole team to use the camera in virtual meetings, as this increases participation and engagement.
- **Schedule some non-work catch-ups**: Use these to give people the space and time to chat more generally. These informal discussions are often the best way to find out the true state of how individuals are coping.
- **Be honest!** Don't be tempted to tell 'fibs' that might catch you out later on, and provide clear and concise communication. Even if your organisation is going through a period of change don't make promises or statements that you later need to retract.
- **Be empathetic and listen:** This is probably the most important factor. Listen to all your team members' points of view and give them clear and constructive information to help them conduct their role in the most effective way.

Recap on remote working

The benefits of a remote team:

- You have access to a wide talent pool!
- You're helping the environment, and so the carbon footprint improves

- Motivation increases, leading to improved productivity
- Less absenteeism
- Employee wellbeing improves

My advice is: be prepared

Preparation is a key theme throughout this book, from preparing for difficult conversations to performance reviews. So, it's no surprise it's here again for creating the best way to manage a remote team.

Take a look at the checklist below and see how you measure up if you're currently managing remote teams or if you plan to manage them in the future:

- ☐ Are your recruitment and onboarding processes set up for remote workers?
- ☐ Does everyone have access to online tools for virtual meetings and chat functions?
- ☐ Hold regular 1-1s and team meetings
- ☐ Set clear deadlines and goals
- ☐ Be mindful of time zones and working hours
- ☐ Do not manage by email
- ☐ Set up a buddy system
- ☐ Encourage a routine for work
- ☐ Set up virtual catch ups and meetings

Here is a mini **checklist** for you, that I've put together to help you with your virtual meetings:

- [ ] Hold virtual team meetings and encourage all team members to have the camera on.
- [ ] Use visual icons such as the hand raise for people to participate.
- [ ] Be clear and concise in your communication.
- [ ] Listen. It's much easier to get distracted when you're on a video call than in person.
- [ ] Practise those verbal nods and sounds to show the other person you're listening.
- [ ] Consider setting up occasional coffee catch-up virtual sessions where NO work is discussed. These become a complete shut-off from business and work. Assign random team members to chat within the chat function or create break-out rooms to just 'chat'. All this will broaden team members' pool of people to interact with and is good for departmental communication.

Tracy-Anne's Tool Kit Takeaways

Managing a virtual team – I have compiled a list of skills and attributes that are required for being a good virtual manager.

Which ones can you clearly demonstrate?

- ☐ Effective communicator
- ☐ Able to build trust
- ☐ Develop team relationships
- ☐ Harness individual strengths of team members
- ☐ Monitor performance
- ☐ Celebrate success
- ☐ Use technology well
- ☐ Lead by example

Evaluate your own skills and attributes to identify the areas you can develop as part of your personal action plan. There is a template below that might help you. Photocopy it, fill it in and take action to be a good remote team manager!

Personal Action Plan

Skill or knowledge area	Specific action	By when	Comments and update

CHAPTER 11

Not Quite the End of the Game

WELL, WE'RE ALMOST at the end, that is unless you took my advice and dipped in at the end, then you're only at the beginning!

However you have approached this book I want to tell you that I have faith in your ability as a manager, whether you're new to this or not, and I believe in you. Just like Mrs Marion Fielder–White and Mr Tong believed in me all those years ago.

My hope is that you pass this onto your teams too. If you keep believing, encouraging, acquiring and sharing new skills and knowledge, you will become masters in your own role, resulting in great personal and professional success. And have a successful and happy team!

Because, when you support and champion individuals, you help them achieve the right mindset, focus and ambition. And maybe, you'll have a 'Ben' or number two who goes on to step up and run their own team or something more.

If you want to know where I would start, my advice is to read Chapter 2, which focuses on communication. Someone I have worked with before is quite blasé about communication and can be frequently heard saying, "They can talk, can't they? Well then, they can communicate". Technically true I suppose.

But here is the thing: communicating well is the foundation of management. Getting your communication strategies honed and crafted is vital. If you want to know what I think, start with that chapter.

However, if you are a dipper in and dipper outer, that is fine too. This book is designed to give you a toolbox of ideas and strategies to use as you develop in your management role.

"A team above all, Above all a team"

You may be curious about my love of rugby, or maybe you wonder if I play rugby. I tried it at school, and I was terrible. So, I gave it a go but decided I would be a supporter, standing on the side lines cheering my favourite team on.

The first team I supported was one my uncle and cousin played in, their work team. That was my first interaction with rugby in a business context. The humour, the teamwork, the literal blood, sweat and tears really helped me appreciate the power of the team. That's not to shy away from the fact that it can be a brutal game! I in fact quite liked the thud of the contact in the scrum, the cauliflower ears, and witnessing the blood pouring down the side of my cousin's head after a tackle. It taught me that achieving true teamwork, companionship, goals, and targets is not easy, but oh so rewarding when everything comes together.

As I said back in Chapter 1, my aim is to help you to avoid people making an **Ass** out of things, stop it all going **Tits up**, and help them kick the **Ball** out of the park. That is why I love coaching, training and mentoring managers.

Go on, **kick your ball**, increase your performance, your team's performance, and believe in yourself. *You have got this, go for it*. I am cheering you along.

And who knows, perhaps one day, we'll meet at a rugby World Cup final, watching England win.

ACKNOWLEDGEMENTS

I WOULD LIKE to thank the following people for their help with the book and for being cheerleaders: Georgia Varjas, Jody Woodbridge, and my editor Mark. To everyone at SWATT books, you know who you are! In particular Sam for supporting me through the process.

To my early draft readers, Alison, David, Jack, Sarah, Neil, and Karen, you know you spurred me on to keep writing! You all made a significant difference in getting this book on the bookshelves and have provided more inspiration for the next one.

The managers and leaders I have worked with and trained over the last few decades, it is always a delight to support you on your journey.

And, finally, my husband Guy, who has been my biggest cheerleader. He gives me tough medicine when I need it, but lifts me up and is my biggest supporter. Without you, none of this would have happened.

Thank you all.

Bibliography

Chapter 2. The Cs of Communication

Be empathetic, page 25

Empathy definition '*the ability to share someone else's feelings or experiences by imagining what it would be like to be in that person's situation.*'

Reference: dictionary.cambridge.org/dictionary/english/empathy

Handling difficult workplace conversations, page 37

RFU values Teamwork, Respect, Enjoyment, Discipline, and Sportsmanship

Reference: englandrugby.com/about-rfu/the-rfu

Chapter 3. Attitude is Everything

Give yourself the gift of confidence, page 44

Ollie Phillips is a former professional English Rugby Union player and was voted the Best Overseas Rugby Player in France in 2011. You can listen to him talk about dealing with Imposter Syndrome on this podcast by The Growth Show.

Reference: anchor.fm/eximius-group/episodes/Dealing-with-imposter-syndrome-with-Ollie-Phillips-and-Nick-Harrington-ep7gr3

What is Imposter Syndrome, page 49

'The Imposter Phenomenon in High Achieving Women: Dynamics and Therapeutic Intervention'

Reference: paulineroseclance.com/pdf/ip_high_achieving_women.pdf

What is Imposter Syndrome, page 50
Ollie Phillips '*I was a rugby hero and a record-breaker, but I still suffered from imposter syndrome.*'
Reference: Quote – telegraph.co.uk/christmas/2019/11/04/ollie-phillips-rugby-hero-record-breaker-still-suffered-imposter

Chapter 4. Becoming a Motivation Maestro

The importance of motivating your team, page 56
According to Inc.Com over 60% of staff leave an organisation because of their manager.
Reference: predictiveindex.com/learn/inspire/resources/surveys-reports/people-management-report/

So how can you become a Motivation Maestro?, page 58
Maslow's hierarchy of needs quote, "..people had five sets of needs, which come in a particular order. As each level of needs is satisfied, the desire to fulfill the next set kicks in."
Reference: bbc.co.uk/news/magazine-23902918

TATTs for a Motivated Team; 5. Learning Opportunities, page 61
Millennials and Generation Z highlight learning opportunities as something key for them.
References:
weforum.org/agenda/2021/05/upskill-engage-gen-z-workplace/
elearningindustry.com/how-millennials-learn-challenges-ld-managers-face-when-training-employees

Chapter 5. The Good, the Bad and the Ugly

Good relationships = enjoyable work, page 70
A significant contributor to workplace stress is psychosocial hazards related to the culture within an organisation, such as poor interpersonal relations and a lack of policies and practices related to respect for workers (Stoewen, The Canadian Veterinary Journal = La Revue Veterinaire Canadienne, 01 Nov 2016)
Reference: positivepsychology.com/positive-relationships-workplace/

The good, the bad, and the ugly of management relationships, page 72
"Some want it to happen, Some wish it would happen, Others make it happen"
Reference: Quote-Michael Jordan businessman and former professional basketball player.

Building Relationships Cultural Checklist, page 78
The Managers' Circle is a supportive group of managers who will champion and support you, with online resources you can use to develop your skills, you can find out more at themanagersmentor. newzenler.com/the-manager-s-circle/

Chapter 6. Decisions, Decisions, Decisions

You won't always get it right, page 90
"Good decisions come from experience, experience comes from making bad decisions"
Reference: Quote-Mark Twain; was an American writer, humourist, entrepreneur, publisher and lecturer.

Types of Decision Making; Everyday decisions, page 91
Image depicting Operational, Tactical and Strategic decisions.
Reference: bbc.co.uk/bitesize/guides/zkdc7nb/revision/1

Where's your mindset at, page 95
Studies have found that decisions made by diverse teams deliver
60 percent better results.
Reference: Study as reported in People Management,
peoplemanagement.co.uk/experts/research/diversity-drives-
better-decisions

Decision-Making Preferences, page 98
The Vroom-Yetton model is designed to help you to identify the
best decision-making approach and leadership style to take,
based on your current situation. It was originally developed by
Victor Vroom and Philip Yetton in their 1973 book, *Leadership and
Decision Making.*
Reference: mindtools.com/pages/article/newTED_91.htm

Decision-making made easier, page 99
Chartered Management Institute (CMI) tips and recommendations
on how to make a decision.
Reference: managers.org.uk/knowledge-and-insights/resource/
decision-making/

Psychological bias in decision-making, page 100
Explanation and examples of psychological bias
Reference: mindtools.com/pages/article/avoiding-psychological-
bias.htm

Decision Making Tools & Techniques, page 107
Edward Debono – Six Thinking Hats and Group Decision Making Game, page 107

Used with well-defined and explicit Return On Investment success in corporations worldwide, Six Thinking Hats is a simple, effective parallel thinking process that helps people be more productive, focused, and mindfully involved. A powerful tool set, which once learned can be applied immediately.

Reference: debonogroup.com/services/core-programs/six-thinking-hats/

Tannenbaum and Schmidt leadership continuum, page 107

Contingency theorists Robert Tannenbaum and Warren Schmidt identified seven leadership styles. They run in a continuum, from rigid authority at one end through to full freedom for your team at the other. This article from mindtools.com looks at each style in turn

Reference: mindtools.com/pages/videos/tannenbaum-schmidt-transcript.htm

Stakeholder analysis, page 107

Stakeholder Analysis is the first step in Stakeholder Management, an important process that successful people use to win support from others.

Managing stakeholders can help you, too, to ensure that your projects succeed where others might fail. This article and video, looks at the crucial first step – Stakeholder Analysis – in more detail.

Reference: mindtools.com/pages/article/newPPM_07.htm

Force field analysis, page 107

When you're making difficult or challenging decisions, it pays to use an effective, structured decision-making technique that will improve the quality of your decisions and increase your chances of success. Force Field Analysis is one such technique and, in this article and in the video, below, we'll explore what it is and how you can use it.

Reference: mindtools.com/pages/article/newTED_06.htm

Data-informed decisions, page 107

Qlik is an Active Intelligence Platform that closes the gaps between data, insights and action with the only cloud platform built for Active Intelligence.

You can read their article on the Essential Steps to making better Data Informed decision here;

Reference: qlik.com/blog/essential-steps-to-making-better-data-informed-decisions

Chapter 7. Stepping Up

Being The Captain or Boss Lady, page 117

"It's not whether you get knocked down, it's whether you get back up"

Reference: Quote -Vince Lombardi was an American football coach he won the first two Super Bowls at the conclusion of the 1966 and 1967 NFL seasons.

Insights – Yale School of Management

https://insights.som.yale.edu/insights/women-arent-promoted-because-managers-underestimate-their-potential?msclkid=3167 4c1fb9a411ec85baf91d12574b5d

Parent-Adult-Child transactions, page 117

Transactional Analysis (TA) is a psychoanalytic theory and method of therapy, developed by Eric Berne during the 1950s. Transactions refer to the communication exchanges between

people. Simply Psychology have written an article called 'Transactional Analysis – Eric Berne'
Reference: simplypsychology.org

Stepping up to a promotion, page 128
To find out more about The Managers' Circle visit the page below.
Reference: themanagersmentor.newzenler.com/the-manager-s-circle/

Psychological safety, page 129
You can find out more about psychological safety from these articles by the Centre for Creative Leadership or Mckinsey & Company who equip people and organisations to unleash sustained performance.
Reference:
ccl.org/articles/leading-effectively-articles/what-is-psychological-safety-at-work/
mckinsey.com/business-functions/people-and-organisational-performance/how-we-help-clients

Chapter 8. Being Successful

TATTs to help you develop a World Cup winning team, page 137
SMART is a well-established tool that you can use to plan and achieve your goals, it's an acronym for; Specific, Measurable, Achievable, Realistic, Timebound. There are lots of resources available for SMART from mindtools.org to the Chartered Institute for Managers (CMI) The reference link I've provided is a checklist from the CMI.
Reference: www.managers.org.uk/wp-content/uploads/2020/03/CHK-231-Setting_Smart_Objectives.pdf

Tracy-Anne's Toolkit Takeaways, page 140
Reference: Designed by Sheridan Webb - The practical training designer (2) Sheridan Webb - The Practical Training Designer | LinkedIn

Emotional Intelligence for managers (EI): What it REALLY means...., page 142
Daniel Goleman's five principal areas of E.I.
References:
Find out more about Daniel by visiting danielgoleman.info/biography/
To learn more about the five principals or components visit verywellmind.com/components-of-emotional-intelligence-2795438

Self-Reflection, page 145
The Berkeley Well-Being Institute defines Self Reflection as "wanting to know why you do the things you do"
Reference: berkeleywellbeing.com/what-is-self-reflection.html

Self-Reflection, page 145
"The definition of insanity is doing the same thing over and over again and expecting a different result"
Reference: Quote – Albert Einstein, Theoretical Physicist.

Experiment with different tools, page 147
For the full range of tools from the CIPD to help with a reflective practice visit
Reference: cipd.co.uk/Images/reflective-practice-guide_tcm18-12524.pdf

Tracy-Anne's Toolkit Takeaways, page 149

FRIDA is a great tool you can use if you're in a challenging situation, to check in and stabilise your feelings.

Reference: Designed by Sheridan Webb – The practical training designer (2) Sheridan Webb – The Practical Training Designer | LinkedIn

Chapter 9. The Gift of Organisation

Organisation=Productivity, page 151

The Eisenhower Matrix – President Eisenhower is said to have arranged his obligations so that only the important and urgent matters came across his desk. The Eisenhower Matrix uses this same principle to sort out the less urgent and important tasks on your list, which you can then delegate or not do at all.

Reference: eisenhower.me/eisenhower-matrix/

Chapter 10. Remote Working – It is not new

The CIPD Mega Trends report 2020, page 163

https://www.cipd.co.uk/Images/working-from-home-1_tcm18-74230.pdf

Contact Tracy-Anne Barker

You can find out more about Tracy-Anne via her website
tabarkerassociates.co.uk

Or to contact her direct, email
Tracy-Anne@tabarkerassociates.co.uk

And you can follow her on LinkedIn at
linkedin.com/in/tracy-anne-barker

The Managers' Circle

The Managers' Circle is a global community supporting managers and business owners to be more confident, less stressed, and happier in their management jobs. The monthly membership helps them to develop their knowledge and management skills, have maximum impact in their roles, and optimise the performance of their teams.

You can find out more here;
themanagersmentor.newzenler.com/the-manager-s-circle/

HOW NOT TO BALLS IT UP | TRACY-ANNE BARKER